Come and See

Come and See

The Transformation of Personal Prayer

David Keller

Morehouse Publishing

an imprint of Church Publishing Incorporated
Harrisburg — New York

Unless otherwise noted, the Scripture quotations contained herein
are from the *New Revised Standard Version* of the Bible, copyright
© 1989 by the Division of Christian Education of the National
Council of Churches of Christ in the U.S.A. Used by permission.
All rights reserved.

Library of Congress Cataloging-in-Publication Data
Keller, David G. R., 1937–
   Come and see: the transformation of personal prayer /
David Keller.
     p.   cm.
   Includes bibliographical references.
   ISBN 978-0-8192-2319-7 (pbk.)
   1. Prayer—Christianity. I. Title.
BV210.3.K455 2009
248.3'2—dc22

2008042523

Cover design by Jennifer Glosser
Interior design by Vicki K. Black

Printed in the United States of America.

Morehouse Publishing
4775 Linglestown Road
Harrisburg, PA 17112

Morehouse Publishing
445 Fifth Avenue
New York, NY 10016

Morehouse Publishing is an imprint of Church Publishing Incorporated.

08 09 10 11 12 13   10 9 8 7 6 5 4 3 2 1

Table of Contents

*For the men and women whose vision created
the Episcopal House of Prayer at
Saint John's Abbey, Collegeville, Minnesota.
And for the hundreds of retreatants
who shared contemplative prayer
and the wisdom of their life experiences with me
while I was Steward of the House of Prayer,
1994–2002.*

*This book is the child of our mutual silence, humor,
questions, conversations, and desire
to become persons of prayer
in the midst of busy and responsible lives.*

Acknowledgments

In *Come and See* I have tried to present what is most fundamental in the Christian path. This simple message has emerged from the crucible of my personal experience as well as study and experience of the timeless aspects of Christian practice, from both eastern and western Christianity.

I have been blessed by many personal mentors and influenced by the writing of many others. For insights into the wisdom of Jesus' Hebrew legacy I am indebted to the writing of Johs. Pedersen, Abraham Joshua Heschel, and Lawrence Kushner.

My mentors and teachers in the New Testament and life in early Christian communities, especially the desert fathers and mothers, in the patristic period, and in the spread of Christianity to the West have included Columba Stewart, OSB, Mary Forman, OSB, Godfrey Diekmann, OSB, Bruno Barnhart, OSB Cam., Pierson Parker, and W. Norman Pittenger. I am grateful for the scholarly writing of Robert Louis Wilken.

My mentors and teachers in the history and experience of Christian meditation and contemplation have included Evelyn Underhill, Esther de Waal, Donald Allchin, W. Norman Pittenger, John Main, OSB, and Thomas Keating, OCSO. My personal spiritual mentor and guide in contemplative living for over twenty years has been Thomas Hand, SJ.

For wisdom and scholarly writing about the riches of Christian life in the Eastern Orthodox churches I am grateful for the writing of Sergius Bulgakov, Elizabeth Behr-Sigel, Paul Evdokimov, Vladimir Lossky, George A. Maloney, Georgios I. Mantzaridis, Panayiotas Nellas, Stelios Ramfos, and John D. Zizioulas. Donald Allchin of Oxford University and the University of Wales reawakened me to the wisdom of Eastern Orthodox theology and prayer and its influence on the formation of the Anglican Church.

All these mentors have helped me understand, practice, and present the message and experiences of the Christian path, but I am responsible for any factual errors or inaccuracies in interpreting their teaching.

Although I have lived with *Come and See* for two decades, Cynthia Shattuck, my editor at Church Publishing, has helped me bring it to life. She saw its promise and helped me organize, simplify, and clarify its message. No author could ask for more. I am grateful to Nancy Roth, a colleague and author, for introducing me to Cynthia.

Dozens of people have read informal versions of *Come and See* over the years, and their comments and suggestions have encouraged me along the way. They are part of this book. Above all, my wife, Emily Wilmer, has blessed me with patient listening to my "latest ideas," with valuable criticism, and with faithful support of my passion to write.

Preface

C ome and See invites you to learn about prayer more from your own experience than from study. You will find a variety of ways to pray here and I invite you to try some of them right away. Stay with each form of prayer you choose long enough to discern whether or not it is suitable for you. I recommend at least a month of daily practice. There is no need to wait until you finish reading the book. In fact, your experiences in prayer will provide a more personal way to listen and respond to what I have written. It will become a conversation.

Everything in *Come and See* comes from what I have learned from my own experiences of prayer and those of my mentors, most of whom I have never met face to face. This demonstrates the glorious power of prayer. It has no limits. Prayer is simply the flow of energy between God and each human being. It is a relationship that unites each of us with God in a way that transforms our vision of other people and the world. The flow of energy in prayer is the womb of love; it becomes the source of every desire, thought, word, and action. In other words, prayer changes the way we live. It is an ongoing process of transformation.

Prayer touches and forms every aspect of our lives. It embraces the whole person and integrates three fundamental ways of seeing and experiencing God: the rational (using the mind), the physical (using the body), and the interior or mystical (using the silent language of the heart). Every person embodies these three "eyes." *Come and See* will provide suggestions for developing each of these dimensions of prayer and setting them in the context of daily living.

Since prayer has no limits, you and I can be connected even though we have never met. We can learn together about prayer from Jesus of Nazareth and his Jewish heritage, Saint Paul and the earliest Christian faith communities, Christian desert mothers and fathers, early contemplative theologians, medieval mystics, and modern mentors in prayer. Although my focus is Christian, my relationship with mentors from other traditions has enlightened and strengthened my prayers as well. We walk through life together and have much to learn from each other. Experiencing our common ground will help us live in peace and solidarity.

Come and See is written for seekers and beginners, recognizing that the "goal" of prayer is not progress or perfection. Since we are always beginners, this book will also be helpful for you if you are already practicing meditation and contemplation. The challenge of prayer is transformation, not "advancement." If you are skeptical about prayer or reluctant to affiliate with a specific faith community, this book will also be useful; the experience of personal prayer is a reliable foundation for Christian living and learning in our busy and stressed-out society. If you find it difficult to believe in God, these insights from Christian experience will show you some common ground in our journey into the mystery of human life.

To sum up, *Come and See* is for people who want to balance their busy lives in a complex world with personal prayer that is more like a feather than a hippopotamus. What is that like? Come and see!

Chapter One

Come and See

As a human being you are a creature with whom God is constantly speaking and you have been created to respond to God's voice in sacred conversation. This conversation takes place each day and in every situation of your life. There is nothing that can keep you from this natural and life-giving experience of God except lack of desire. Even then God remains within and all around you, speaking and inviting you to respond, but without your response the lure of divine love is incomplete. You have been created to participate in this love, and in the dynamic relationship of genuine conversation, God will reveal to you the most fundamental aspect of your being. You were born to pray.

The foundation of this conversation is the variety of ways God is already present in your life and your desire to be in the company of God. This mutual *presence* will shape your life if you remain open and attentive. It is the intimate environment where you will discover your true self and become one with God.

The essence and practice of personal prayer is your stewardship of this sacred *presence* and *conversation.* Every desire, thought, word, and action flows from this. Your life will reflect what is taking place within you, one day at a time.

WALKING

Prayer is a journey.

Every person asks questions, consciously or unconsciously: "Where have I come from?"; "Who am I?"; "Why am I here?"; and "Where am I going?" All religious traditions seek answers to these questions. Mentors, sacred writings, and theology can be faithful guides, but even inspired teaching has limits when it comes to responding to questions about the mystery of human life. We yearn for wisdom that includes but is not limited to what our minds may comprehend. Our questions point toward a need for *experience* as well as information. The path of personal prayer leads toward awareness and experience of our divine origin, our true identity, and the eternal dimension of our lives. Rather than contemplating "answers," I want to offer you suggestions for contemplative experience of God's presence and disciplines for listening to God's Spirit within us.

How do we walk the path of personal prayer? In Matthew's gospel Jesus of Nazareth describes a fundamental aspect of prayer: "But whenever you pray, go into your room and shut the door and pray to your Father who is in secret; and your Father who sees in secret will reward you" (Matthew 6:6). This "inner room" is the presence of God within us, the origin of our yearning and questions. It is a place where we can be alone with God without the preconceptions, comparisons, and expectations that we or others place upon us. In John's gospel, Jesus also speaks about what takes place in the inner room: "If you continue in my word, you are truly my disciples; and you will know the truth, and the truth will make you free" (John 8:31–32). It is possible to experience that truth personally, as well as to know the freedom to discover our true identity. Henri Nouwen once said, "Where true inner freedom is, there is God.

And where God is, there we want to be." With these words he sums up the attraction of our "inner room." The presence of God is a place of complete freedom and every human being has a passion to be free. This is why we desire God. We yearn for authenticity, truth, and the freedom to be ourselves. All praying, whether it is in our inner room or the middle of a crowd, is telling God, "I want to be where you are!"

As we have seen, prayer is a unique environment for experiencing God and having a sacred conversation. This mutual presence and conversation is the source of all theology because theology is about experiencing God. A wise fourth-century monk named Evagrius Ponticus said, "If you are a theologian you truly pray. If you truly pray you are a theologian." In other words, we can only speak about what we have experienced. But what leads us to that experience?

An incident in the first chapter of John's gospel describes an encounter of two disciples of John the Baptist with Jesus. As usual, the evangelist sows a simple event with seeds of wisdom. As Jesus approaches, John the Baptist declares to his followers, "Look, here is the Lamb of God!" As the two men approach Jesus, he asks them, "What are you looking for?" The men ask, "Rabbi, where are you staying?" and Jesus responds with, "Come and see" (John 1:35–39).

This short encounter describes the internal restlessness that begins the journey we share with every other human being. An inner and very natural yearning of the spirit attracted the two men to the preaching and baptism of John the Baptist, but he directs their search beyond himself to Jesus. The journey always begins with a longing for "something." We sense incompleteness within ourselves.

As the men approach Jesus, he discerns their spiritual longing. The question "What are you looking for?"

awakens endless possibilities. The journey begins with a conversation, not answers or promises. Jesus will not impose himself on the restlessness of the young men. They sense this freedom and want to continue the journey.

"Rabbi, where are you staying?" articulates an intuitive sense that Jesus is a link to the "something" they desire. Their attraction to him reflects his own deeply rooted wisdom and vitality. They want to know more. They realize his physical presence expresses an internal presence. They want to find where this presence dwells and where Jesus' spirit is rooted and fed.

Once again, Jesus invites the two men further into a journey that is both physical and beyond words. "Come and see" leaves room for the freedom and risk to accompany Jesus toward the mystery they desire. It is a mutual journey. Jesus will neither coerce the men nor make the journey for them. He invites them into a relationship that will lead them to the home they are seeking.

Jesus' invitation will evoke a unique response from each one of us, yet it will lead us all to a growing and abiding relationship with God. As we take time to enter the "inner room" to which Jesus invites us, we will begin to discover our origin, true identity, and the life we are created to live, both now and ever afterward.

PRESENCE

Prayer is an encounter.

Every relationship begins with presence. Each person must "show up" and experience the other in order for a process of bonding to begin. This simple act allows listening to take place at several different levels—from body language and speech to a more subtle inner language without thoughts or words.

Soon after becoming a priest I lived for twelve years among the Ingalik tribe of the Athabascan Indians in the

Yukon River valley of central Alaska. My first home was a small log cabin in the village of Shageluk on the Innoko River, a tributary of the Yukon. The population was about one hundred fifty and the nearest road that connected with a highway system was over three hundred miles away. Although the Episcopal Church had been present in the area for one hundred years, I was the first resident Episcopal priest in Shageluk, a New Jersey boy learning to live in a culture that was miles away from my own in more ways than one.

Fortunately, I had good mentors who shared their rich way of life with competence, patience, and humor. During my first winter, Raymond, my next door neighbor, taught me the basics of "driving" a dog team and using a chain saw. One day I was trying to split wood and Raymond came out of his house and said, "David, if we ever get TV in our village we won't need it for laughs. We'll just watch you splitting wood!" Then he showed me a better way and probably saved me from chopping off my foot. Late in the fall, just before the temperature dropped below zero and the wind began blowing snow into tall drifts, Grandpa Robert came to see me as I stood on the river bank. He said, "David, if you treat the weather as an enemy to be conquered you will not last long here. Don't fight it. Let it be a friend and teach you what is possible and what you must do to get along. Then you will live here a long time."

Raymond and Robert took time to share practical wisdom with me so that I could survive in that extreme and sometimes dangerous environment. It was the early 1960s and a time of radical social change for small villages in Alaska. Over the years we continued to be present to each other in a myriad of ways that included hauling wood, fishing, hunting, community development projects, worship, laughter, playing pinochle, tragedy, tears, sharing Christian and indigenous religious experiences, as well as conflict, misunderstandings, and reconciliations. Our evolving friendship was rooted in trusting the reliability and integrity of each other's presence.

The culture of the Ingalik people is based on the power of mutual presence. Community and interdependence are fundamental patterns in their lives. When you see someone on the trail or enter their home you say, "Ah-deh!" The other person replies, "Goh-geh-deh!" The encounter begins with "I am here!" and is made complete with "I am here, too!" I have learned that this simple exchange also describes the heart of prayer. Prayer is nothing more than being present to God and trusting that God is present, too. "I am here!" "So am I!" Teresa of Avila, a sixteenth-century Spanish Carmelite saint, taught that prayer is nothing more than taking time to be with a Friend who we know loves us. Like any friendship, prayer is not easy, nor is it always emotionally satisfying. It can be filled with long periods of silence and doubt when we wonder, is anyone else there?

During my first year in Shageluk it was hard for me to get into the rhythm of the way people visit and have conversations. Someone would come to my cabin and after an initial greeting we would sit in silence. Initially it was very uncomfortable for me. Finally I learned that my feeble attempts to create conversation were not necessary. The visitor just wanted to be with me for a while and would get up and say, "Well, I'll go now." I learned, too, that conversations took more time because people paused longer between statements. Silence was a time for listening to something beyond mere physical presence and words. As I look back on these early visits in Shageluk I am reminded of an incident in the life of one of the early Christian desert fathers of Egypt. An archbishop came to visit Abba Pambo at his hermitage in Scetis. They sat in silence until some of the monks present asked Abba Pambo to speak to the archbishop. Abba Pambo said, "If he is not edified by my silence, he will not be edified by my speech."

Being present to God is not a static relationship. Something happens and something is shared. It is a mutual presence. We and God are not only present; we bring and share a "presence." You may be familiar with the biblical account of Jacob, the grandson of Abraham, wrestling all night with an angel at the River Jabbok. Wrestling is a radical form of presence! When Jacob got the upper hand, his opponent knocked Jacob's hip out of joint and demanded that Jacob release him. But Jacob said, "I will not let you go until you bless me."

Although this is an unconventional way to end a wrestling match, in Jacob's Hebrew culture a blessing was not simply a gesture of approval or a desire for another's well-being. The Hebrews believed the human soul was saturated with power, present both within a person as well as in her or his words, actions, and influence. No person can live without this life-giving power, which is called *berakha* or "blessing." When God blesses, God bestows sacred and life-giving power.

For Christians, this sacred power is known as "grace." The Hebrews believed that God's blessing completes our creation and makes us a "living soul." Soul includes every aspect of our lives — body and mind as well as spirit. Under a canopy of stars, in a remote wrestling ring, Jacob sensed a mysterious presence and power in his opponent and would not let him go: "And there he blessed him. So Jacob called the place Peniel [the face of God], saying, 'For I have seen God face to face, and yet my life is preserved'" (Genesis 32:29–30).

Jacob's mysterious opponent was not only present; his very being affected the surrounding environment. The Hebrews called this influence a person's *counsel.* Counsel is the way in which someone shows forth the sacred power of God's blessing through interacting with the world outside, a blessing intended for the common good. I have often been in a room when someone enters whose presence changes the chemistry of the whole room, regardless of how many others are there. In the four gospels there are incidents where people recognized the unique divine "presence" in Jesus' words and actions. "Now when Jesus had finished saying these things, the crowds were astounded at his teaching, for he taught them as one having authority, and not as their scribes" (Matthew 7:28–29). I have experienced this same presence equally in the company of spiritual leaders and poets and musicians, but it is not limited to them. How many times has a child stolen your heart? How many times has a stranger's presence changed the whole atmosphere of a meeting for the better, or an elder's quiet wisdom or simple action changed your outlook on a situation?

But presence does not rely only on words to change or create an environment for good or ill. Presence is the manifestation of a living soul and includes the fullness of being. Although I have emphasized the positive effects of presence, it can be used also to manipulate and dominate others when its purpose is to control outcomes and results. We all have the freedom to misuse God's blessing in the interest of our own self-aggrandizement; in more extreme cases we may cause emotional or physical harm. Negative presence makes true conversation almost impossible and thrives on coercion and intimidation, and we are all capable of it. There have been times in my life when my presence has been a gift and blessing, but I am painfully aware that at other times it has caused pain and misunderstanding. It is not easy to be stewards of the blessing that makes us living souls. We are always beginners and God's faithful presence offers opportunities for the blessing to be made new in the environment of personal prayer.

Recently my wife, Emily, received an invitation to a friend's birthday party. It ended with this request, "Please, no gifts. Only your presence is requested." Her friend wants more than Emily's physical presence. She desires Emily. God is continually offering invitations for our presence. How shall we respond and what will happen?

THE MANY FACES OF PRESENCE

I am an amateur astronomer and own a large sophisticated telescope. When I gaze into the mystery of distant galaxies and nebulae, the eyepiece becomes a sanctuary filled with divine presence. Words limit the experience; there is only Presence. Thousands of years ago the same dark canopy of deep space led a psalmist to declare: "The heavens are telling the glory of God.... There is no speech, nor are there words; their voice is not heard; yet their voice goes out through all the earth" (Psalm 19:1–4). The presence of this unknowable aspect of God initiates a mutual seeing and I am no longer the same. I experience powerful awe, a fear that lures me *toward* divine mystery and invites me to drop to my knees, knowing I am a creature and not the center of the universe. The starry night keeps me from taking myself too seriously and wanting to limit God to what my mind or experience may comprehend.

Sometimes God's presence is beyond words or concepts, shrouded in mystery. At other times we experience God as a companion. I have had moments when God's presence is so palpable I feel as though I am the only person in the universe upon whom God's gaze and concern are focused. Several years ago I was hiking in Israel near the high rock cliffs of Arbel above the Sea of Galilee near Magdala. As I climbed the rock face toward an ancient synagogue built into a cave, an eagle left its nest and dove toward the base of the cliff, pulling up at the last minute and spreading its wings like a canopy. My thoughts immediately turned to an image in the fortieth chapter of the book of the prophet Isaiah. He declares that even though God's "understanding is unsearchable" (40:28), God cares intimately for the tired, faint, and weary. Isaiah compares God's intimacy with that of a mother eagle, who knows the time when an eaglet must learn to fly. She will nudge it from her high nest into a free fall that forces the eaglet to use its wings for the first time. The small, vulnerable eaglet could be dashed to pieces if its strength is not up to its maiden flight. But at a critical moment its mother, also in a free fall, soars beneath the eaglet with outstretched wings, ready to lift her child to safety if the eaglet's strength fails. In response to the children of Israel's complaints that God no longer cared about them, Isaiah reminds his faith community that "those who wait for the LORD shall renew their strength, they shall mount up with wings like eagles, they shall run and not be weary, they shall walk and not faint" (40:31). Isaiah's words speak to the doubts of our modern world as well. When I am tempted to be cynical over what appears to be God's absence in my life or in society, the One who is beyond my knowledge says, "Listen to me in silence..." (Isaiah 41:1).

In the late 1970s I was a volunteer chaplain at a state prison. Each week I spent half a day with inmates in the maximum security unit, celebrating the Eucharist and having conversations with them. Each week I looked forward to being with them. There was an inmate in solitary confinement who had been convicted of a hideous murder. Through the unofficial communication process that is part of every prison culture, the inmates who participated in the Eucharist asked the warden to let me visit the man in solitary. Although visitors were not permitted, the warden agreed. As I waited in a secure visitor's room with a guard present, I wondered what I could say to this man. When he was brought into the room I asked the guard to leave so that we could speak in confidence. The guard agreed, but remained outside the door looking through a glass window. We sat in silence for an eternity. Finally I said, "Is there something I can do for you?" After another long silence, during which we maintained eye contact, he said, "There is nothing you can do. I just wanted to be with you." We spent the rest of the time in silence until the guard entered the room and ended the visit. The man in solitary confinement wanted to be with another human being. He wanted my presence, and that was enough. I will never know what prompted the need for my visit; it was unspoken, but significant. My presence was enough.

We are tempted to use prayer as a time for thinking, in the hope it will be a "productive" use of our time, but prayer is not a time for thinking. It is a time for presence. Thinking is an integral part of human nature, but it is not our highest or most essential activity. The purpose of prayer is not intense self-reflection or progress in our spiritual life so much as an opportunity to be *present and alert* to God and other human beings.

I will never forget a woman who arrived for a silent retreat I once led. She was an executive in a large financial management corporation who needed a weekend break from her busy and responsible job. During supper on the first evening she asked me what the retreat would be like. As I described the pattern of chanting and long periods of silent meditation that would take place over the weekend, she turned pale and said, "I chose this retreat because this is the only break in my schedule for a long time. I had no idea it was a silent retreat. I'm embarrassed because I did not read the flyer more carefully. I have no idea what I should do during all this silence. Actually, I'm very nervous. Perhaps I should have a good laugh at myself and just drive home after supper." I encouraged her to give it a try and wait until Saturday afternoon before making a decision about leaving. We agreed to meet privately during the retreat so she could "check in."

Although she stayed for the whole weekend, it was not easy. She was not comfortable with an experience she could not define and did not seem to have a logical outcome. There was nothing to pray "for" and no apparent purpose. Yet at the end of the retreat she surprised me and the other retreatants by saying, "This silent retreat was an amazing and unexpected experience for me. In all my years of being raised a Roman Catholic and my thirty-three years as an Episcopalian, I never knew you could hang out with God. Somehow, our religion is failing us on that matter. It has become a passive religion rather than an active one." In other words, during this weekend of unexpected silence a very busy and productive executive had experienced a simple sense of presence, and that turned out to be enough. She spent the weekend doing what a Teresa of Avila might have called "hanging out with God," although Teresa put it a little differently: "Prayer is nothing else than an intimate sharing between friends; it means taking time frequently to be alone with him who, we know, loves us."

Prayer is a reminder that our primary vocation, as human beings, is to enter into the very life of God. It is a timeless presence—within time and space—where we *experience* the transcendent being of God, who is love. In personal prayer we place ourselves, intentionally and with openness, in the presence of the One who is the heart of reality. The daily practice of prayer is a choice to commit our lives to what is most fundamental. This mutual presence with and experience of God becomes the source of our love and the wisdom that guides our actions and relationships.

In the late third century, thousands of men and women began to leave the cities and towns of the Roman

Empire and form small communities in the deserts of the eastern part of the Mediterranean world. They began a movement whose life of prayer and wisdom are the roots of Christian monastic spirituality. One of these desert elders said, "If our inner self behaves soberly, it can control the outer self; but if the inner self does not do this, what other means is there of controlling the tongue?"[1] Abba Poemen, another dweller in the desert, said, "Teach your heart to follow what your tongue is saying." In speaking of our tendency to say one thing and do another, he taught, "Men try to appear excellent in preaching, but they are less excellent in practicing what they preach."

There are times when I wonder whether my periods of silent meditation are worthwhile and productive. So often they "come up empty." Most of the time I am unaware of any direct result from my prayers. But after decades of periods of daily silence in God's presence, I have learned to trust that something *is happening* at a deep level of the mystery of who I am. There is a part of me that only silence can touch. The "inside" of me is gradually being formed as my heart listens quietly to God's faithful presence. The gift of this presence is that I am not responsible for the outcome, not in control, as I am being formed quietly and slowly. To be a disciple means both "to follow" and "to remain in the presence." As the desert elders learned, the person I am becoming on the inside of my life will gradually begin to influence my exterior words and actions.

The practice of personal prayer places our lives in the hands of the One who "laid the foundations of the world and all that is in it" (Psalm 89:11, BCP). It helps us walk in the light of God's presence, whose energies bring forth righteousness and justice and whose foundation is love and truth. When I am able to place my life in God's hands day after day, I begin to see myself and my neighbor from the perspective of God's love for the world. If I let go of my desire to control everything around me, I gradually begin to desire what is best for other people. This love is not prompted by fear, a hoped-for reward, or society's rules. It becomes the desire of my heart through the unconditional love I am experiencing in God's silent presence. As Evelyn Underhill, the Anglican writer and mystic, described it, "There is a deep foundation of silence in each of us in which the eternal Word is born. And therein lies our vocation: to listen to that Word and to live thereby."[2]

The two most fundamental aspects of personal prayer are: *the presence of God* and *attentiveness to that presence*. It is a mutual seeing. There are only two prerequisites for presence: *desire and persistence*. I must "show up." One reason we often give up on personal prayer is that it is hard work and requires difficult decisions about the use of our time. Hanging out with God is not easy, especially when I demand results or let my mind and activities become scattered. The key is to follow my desire for God, not to achieve mastery. We have to remember that we are always beginners in the constant call to pray. As the Benedictine writer John Main memorably puts it, "The call to meditate is an invitation to stop leading our lives on the basis of second-hand evidence."[3] Perhaps the most difficult aspect of being in God's presence is the realization that no one else can do it for us!

Chapter Two

Dancing with God

The early Christian teachers, preachers, and pastors were steeped in contemplative prayer and meditation. Their theology flowed from reflection on their experience of God. Their response was a great *enthusiasm* for God: the word "enthusiasm" comes from the Greek *en theos*, meaning "in God." They often used the image of dancing to describe their mystical life-giving experiences of God. When music and a dancer's movement are combined to create a dance, each is changed and affected by the other's presence. Each is transformed as the music and the steps of the dance permeate each other and become one. In the same way the simple process of personal prayer is a mutual sharing of presence, a sacred dance. We offer the gift of our presence and God offers the same gift in return. The result is mutual love and in this reciprocity both we and God experience a self-giving which is the threshold of union, a "new creation," in the words of Saint Paul (2 Corinthians 5:17).

Paul had a vivid awareness of being united with Christ. It was not a theological perception or idea, but something he experienced at the heart of his being—a new dimension permeating every aspect of his life. He said, "It is no longer I who live, but it is Christ who lives in me" (Galatians 2:20). The way this happens to you and me is truly a mystery, because it is not something we can achieve on our own. It is a gift that Christian poets and theologians have tried to articulate for two thousand years. Early Christians called it *theosis* or "deification." Both words refer to sharing the life of God within the limitations of our humanity, and they are based on the passage in 2 Peter where the writer proclaims that God's promises to us include becoming "participants of the divine nature" (1:4).

Pseudo-Macarius, a Syrian monk of the fourth century, describes this transformation in a sermon using the image of the sun to describe our participation in God. He does not say that you or I *become* God, but that each of us becomes fully human when we participate in the nature of God. The sun is a single star whose inner and intense nuclear fusion gives birth to billions of photons (individual units of light) that, in turn, give life to our solar system. Each photon is unique, yet it carries and radiates the intrinsic energy and nature of its source. Macarius continues:

> Thus the soul is completely illumined with the unspeakable beauty of the glory of the light of the face of Christ and is perfectly made a participator of the Holy Spirit. It is privileged to be the dwelling-place and the throne of God, all eye, all light, all face, all glory and all spirit, made so by Christ who drives, guides, carries, and supports the soul about and adorns and decorates the soul with his spiritual beauty.[4]

The more receptive we (or our instruments) become to receiving the energy of the observed light, the more we learn about the characteristics of the light's source — in this case the sun. When Marcarius speaks of the soul being "completely illumined" by "the light of the face of

Christ," he is affirming our need to be fully open, through prayer, to the movement of the Holy Spirit.

The audacity of this theologian is hard to believe, and yet he is merely supplying us with an almost forgotten strand of the simple and positive message of the Christian path: we are sacred beings created to manifest the likeness of God. That is our authentic nature. It is who we are! This does not deny the consequences of our weaknesses and fallibility. Yet it stands in unapologetic contrast to the popular cynicism and fatalism about human nature that result from our irresponsible treatment of each other and the earth. Although we cannot rely on ourselves to create ourselves, Saint Paul reminds us that we *can* rely on God to give birth to our authentic nature. "May the God of peace himself sanctify you entirely; and may your spirit and soul and body be kept complete and blameless at the coming of our Lord Jesus Christ. The one who calls you is faithful, and he will do this" (1 Thessalonians 5:23–24).

Both Saint Paul and Pseudo-Macarius remind us of who we really are! How do we accept and live into this truth about ourselves? How do we place ourselves in the hands of the One who calls us and is faithful?

The roots of Christian contemplative prayer and meditation lie in the life and ministry of Jesus of Nazareth and his Jewish heritage. The gospels are filled with references to his pattern of quiet reflection and meditation. The power and wisdom of his active involvement in his Jewish religious community and in the society that surrounded him had their source in his passionate openness to God's presence. It is clear that Jesus experienced a union with God that he knew was fundamental for authentic and abundant human life. He expressed this union with no hesitation or ambiguity:

The Father and I are one. (John 10:30)

My teaching is not mine but his who sent me.
(John 7:16)

Very truly, I tell you, the Son can do nothing on
his own, but only what he sees the Father doing.
(John 5:19)

Jesus desired this same union for all persons, praying
"that they be one, as we are one" (John 17:11). Furthermore, he knew that his experience of life was what
God desired for all human beings: "I came that they may
have life, and have it abundantly" (John 10:10).

Contemplative prayer and meditation are opportunities for us to experience this same authentic and abundant human life. They are simple and normal ways for
us to be who we really are, and require nothing but our
desire to be present to God. Yet this simplicity takes
much courage in a society that above all values productivity and control. Therefore we are reluctant to place
ourselves in God's hands and become vulnerable to
transformation. We fear extending the borders of our experience beyond the safety of what we can manage all
on our own.

The executive who learned she could "hang out with
God" took the risk of extending the boundaries of her
experience of prayer. Faced with a weekend of silence,
her first impulse was to take control of the situation by
opting out of it and going home. I wish I could say I have
always been as honest as she was about my life of prayer.
So often I turn away from change, challenge, or even
boredom, kicking and screaming all the way! I want to
stay where it is safe in my life with God. With the best intentions I try to tell God what the world needs and how
God should fix things. Sometimes I am reluctant to listen to God because I might hear an invitation or challenge that requires risk or a courageous response on my
part. God often says, "David, you and every human

being have everything necessary to create a just and compassionate society. Don't blame me. Depend on me!"

Why do I have these problems in prayer? Basically, it is an *attitude* problem. Jesus said, "Take my yoke upon you, and learn from me; for I am gentle and humble in heart, and you will find rest for your souls" (Matthew 11:29). Jesus reminds me that the primary foundation for prayer is humility, rooted in the depth of my heart. It is my attitude that makes prayer and experience of God possible. I must shift my gaze away from myself and my life; in prayer I must be prepared to let go of the self I work so hard to create and accept that I am a creature of God. The attitude of letting go will transform my personal prayer, the core of my relationship with God and therefore of my relationships with my neighbors.

The attitude of "dying to self" begins in my heart, the seat of my being. It is the place where my true self lives and where God's presence lives within me. When my heart is soft and flexible it will expand and make more room for the One who is already there. I have learned that a humble heart is one that knows it is a creature of God and responds in gratitude, wonder, and love. This attitude is different from the conventional wisdom of today's society, which values control, security, and self-interest. Contrary to popular opinion, civility, listening to conflicting points of view, and being open to correction are not signs of weakness. Civility, sensitive listening, and humility are manifestations of compassion flowing from a flexible heart. They are the fruit of experience of God in prayer.

The heart of the Christian path is learning to manifest the presence of God, who is already in us, through our manner of life. Our vocation is to make Christ *tangible.* The earliest Christians knew that this vocation is rooted and nurtured in the wisdom of the Bible, personal prayer, and the sacramental life of the Christian community.

Although the early theologians of the Christian church were learned in Greek and Roman philosophy and literature, they were different from other philosophers and thinkers of their day. Their unique thought flowed from the three spiritual wells mentioned above: prayer, the Bible, and the sacraments, especially the Eucharist. Some of them spoke of the Christian path as a journey toward union with God, describing it with the Greek word *perichoresis*. The Greek *peri* (literally "surrounding" or "with"), when used with *choresis* ("dance" or "dancing"), means "dancing in relation to another." What pushes us toward this dance? The initiative for this union is grace. All human beings who open themselves to the movement of God's grace can become participants in the dance.

LISTENING TO THE MUSIC

There are many voices competing for our attention in the world today—our families, our coworkers, the homeless and hungry, our politicians. We hear voices hounding us to buy more goods and services, voices instilling fear, hopeful voices, cynical voices, vengeful voices, our own voice of self-preservation. Which voices will we heed? Which words will become the springboards of our action and the source of our vision? I know how easy it is to become torn and scattered in a world of constant and often conflicting voices. My vision may become blurred with such competition for my heart. There are times when I feel imprisoned and voiceless in the midst of the endless demands for my commitment and loyalty. With so much demanding my attention and needing resolution, I often wonder where my place is. I sometimes feel helpless and powerless in the wake of the world's needs. I must have the courage to stay the course when Jesus invites me, saying, "Make my word your home."

It all begins in the silence of being present to God. The venue is my open and listening heart. Jesus said, "Out of the heart, the mouth speaks." My goal is not success in holiness. It is longing to be faithful to the truth of Jesus' words, regardless of the outcome. In the silence of prayer I have learned the meaning of perfect freedom, the only source of joy. It is what Jesus described as "abundant life," but it is not a "possession." Gregory of Nyssa, an early Christian mystic, bishop, and theologian of the church, learned from his own experience that life with God is never fully defined or completed; he speaks of the soul "continually making fresh discoveries." God's love for us is always expanding before our eyes and our desire for God is a never-ending journey. Prayer is a limitless vocation to live deeper and deeper into the mystery of God and our own authentic humanity. It is living with enthusiasm, in God.

Hanging out with God and *remaining* in God's company are the only ways to embrace a life that is free and full. Prayer keeps me rooted in God as the dance goes on in the busyness of a chaotic world.

Chapter Three

Roots

Personal prayer roots us in the experience of God and shows us how to see the world through God's eyes. When this becomes a daily pattern, our words and actions will not be scattered or lose their power because they will become part of the context of God's desires for the world. We will sense an amazing freedom, knowing the outcome of each day's living is in God's hands. This freedom will not lead us away from the world but, on the contrary, engage us ever more deeply in the life of the world by showing us what is authentic, fundamental, and life-giving. Prayer takes us from the surface of life into its sacred roots and helps us discern actions and situations that are just, responsible, caring, and generative.

When we are rooted in God we are led across a threshold where we encounter and *become* the words, actions, and very consciousness of our true home, Jesus, who is as much alive today as he was in the first century. This home is never a haven *from* the world but a place where you and I are constantly formed and reformed as we cross and re-cross the threshold between contemplation and action. It is a place where we are very close to God, a place where "the LORD is your keeper; the LORD is your shade at your right hand. The sun shall not strike you by day, nor the moon by night. The LORD will keep you from all evil; he will keep your life" (Psalm 121:5–7).

I know myself well enough to realize I cannot produce or master the qualities of authentic human life on my own. They do not exist in some otherworldly supermarket or on eBay, to be placed in my holiness shopping basket. The qualities of authentic human life are sacred gifts, the fruits of my naked openness to the movement of God's Spirit in my heart. I will know their presence when they become manifest in my daily work and relationships and when they enrich the lives of other people. These gifts are *humility, fidelity, courage, perseverance, a willingness to be led, patience,* and *trust.* There are other gifts, but these are plenty for a beginner like me.

EXPERIENCE OF GOD IS THE TAP ROOT

Christians are often called "the people of the book," referring to the central role the Bible has in our tradition. I disagree. Although our roots are firmly planted in the rich soil of the Bible, our identity lies in our experience of God. We are formed by our experience of Jesus. The words and wisdom of the Bible, our creeds, and our theology proceed from experience of God and reflect the influence of that experience in the ways we approach life and try to live. The encounter with God in Jesus has called together and formed the various faith communities within the Christian church. Our common vocation is to make our experience of God tangible in our lives. We are called to make the image of God, our natural goodness, manifest in our words, relationships, and actions. Jesus said that we will be known by our love, not by our words. This is easier said than done.

As we have seen, the earliest Christians, whether living in the busyness and complexities of city life or in the simplicity of desert caves and small monastic communities, shared a vision of human life that reflects the image of the One who made us. But they also knew from their own experience how easy it is for any of us to go off on our own, to lose sight of that image and create ourselves in our own image. Rather than trying to remake their lives after God's likeness, they often made choices that fragmented and dissipated their lives, as well as bringing harm to others and to themselves.

At the same time, they struggled to "walk the talk" and did not isolate themselves from other people and the needs of the world. These desert-dwellers were "streetwise," living each day with the anxieties, temptations, and challenges of human life. Their experience of God affirmed their vision that the original and natural integrity of each human life is rooted in the image of God. Even the hermits, though physically separate from everyone else, were connected to others through their prayer, offerings, and sharing of wisdom. Others in their communities fed the hungry, tended the sick, and were substantively involved in the political and theological debates of their day. They were ordinary people, like you and me, following Jesus' call to make their words and actions holy, congruent with the image of God. How can you and I in turn make God's image tangible in the way we live?

I have learned how easy it is to create myself in the image of my own hopes and fears while ignoring the divine image that is my authentic self. The journey from recognizing the image of God in me to actually manifesting the likeness of God is neither easy nor automatic. The early Christians learned that self-knowledge and honesty are crucial though difficult necessities in our journey toward becoming authentic human beings. Therefore, they were careful about the way they lived and were conscious of malign influences that could distract them from their desire to love God and their neighbors. As we have seen, they depended on contemplation, the Bible, and the Eucharist as their threefold source of divine spiritual nurture and power. This combination kept them rooted in God and at home in the words of Jesus. As Saint Teresa of Avila reminds us, "The Lord desires intensely that we love him and seek his company."

The need to seek God's company is why personal prayer is essential for every Christian; it is one of the primary sources of our experience of God. Our collective experiences of God form our faith communities as the body of Christ. Personal prayer, whether contemplation or meditation, is the venue where God forms us as Christians and empowers us to love the world as God loves the world. It is easy to forget or devalue the wisdom of past generations and, sadly, Christian churches today often fail to mentor their members in the richness of our own traditions of personal prayer. While we have much to learn from the wisdom and practices of other religious traditions, we should not overlook the substantive disciplines of Christian spiritual formation that can challenge and transform our lives.

Thomas Traherne, a seventeenth-century English pastor, poet, and mystic, called personal prayer, the Bible, and the sacraments God's "little trinity," an artery through which we are fed by the energy of God's grace and Spirit. His wisdom, like all the great Christian mystics, writers, teachers, and activists from a variety of traditions, echo the experiences of the earliest Christians. In their search for God they developed patterns of contemplative prayer and disciplines of meditation. These forms of prayer were called "ascetic disciplines." The Greek word *askesis* means "exercise, training," while the Roman root for the word "discipline" is *disciplina,* from *discipulus,* or "disciple." Thus ascetic disciplines are forms of knowledge and practices that help us to care for something we value. In order to be a "disciple" we must be willing to cultivate a desire for listening and place ourselves in an environment for listening.

In its earliest life, the Christian community placed great emphasis on caring for our souls through various patterns of listening to God, the Bible, ourselves, Christian mentors and teachers, and the world. These ascetic disciplines, however, are not ends in themselves. Rather, they help us care for our souls as we journey from first recognizing the image of God in ourselves to showing forth the likeness of God in the way we live. Ascetic disciplines, especially contemplative prayer and meditation, help us take time to listen and be watchful for the movement of God's Spirit in us. They place us in an attitude of *vulnerability*, open to spiritual growth and transformation. They school us in the work of love: God's love for us and our love of our neighbors. The desert fathers and mothers called this "guarding the soul" from danger. They were aware of all the different influences and temptations that can lead us away from the path toward spiritual transformation. Our life of personal praying, worship in our faith community, and our pattern of ascetical disciplines (a "rule of life") work together for the stewardship of our thoughts, words, actions, bodies, minds, spirits, and the common good of our neighbors and the earth.

PRAYER IN THE EARLY CHURCH

A fourth-century desert father, Abba Isaac, summarized the teaching of Saint Paul on personal prayer. Isaac describes the discipline of praying as a combination of supplications, prayers, intercessions, and thanksgivings. A supplication, he says, is "an imploring or a petition concerning sins, by which a person who has been struck by compunction begs for pardon for his present or past misdeeds." Isaac thought that this kind of prayer was for beginners, who are more likely to be "harassed by the stings and by the memory of their vices." The second discipline, which he calls simply "prayers," are a way of making a vow to God. For example, "we pray when we renounce this world and pledge that, dead to every earthly deed and to an earthly way of life, we will serve the Lord with utter earnestness of heart." Intercessions, the third form of prayer, are undertaken on behalf of others, fervently "beseeching on behalf of our dear ones and for the peace of the whole world." Fourth and last, Isaac lists thanksgiving for what God has done for us in the past and present as well as "foreseeing what great things God has prepared for those who love him."[5]

Why should supplications be "first of all"? Abba Isaac speaks from personal experience. Awareness of vices and sins can be a serious barrier to our relationship with God. Sometimes it is hard to pray when we are "harassed" by these memories, especially if we are new to prayer or have given up on it. Isaac urges us to let awareness of sins coupled with "compunction" (genuine sorrow for "present or past misdeeds") become our prayer. As difficult as it may be, this supplication will free us to expand our experience of prayer and grow in love of ourselves, others, and God. Isaac must have remembered Jesus' words: "But the one to whom little is forgiven, loves little" (Luke 7:47). The simple prayer "Lord, have mercy" expresses both sorrow for sin and a profound desire for restored union with God. God's mercy is present even before we ask for it, but it is our sense of alienation that prompts our prayer in the first place.

It is important to realize that in the Bible and in the experiences of the desert elders like Abba Isaac, mercy is not condescension. God's mercy is God's compassionate desire to be with each of us in solidarity, regardless of what we have done. Mercy is not revocation of punishment; it is faithful presence and mutual love in the midst of weakness, pain, and anxiety. The source of mercy is the heart. The act of saying "Lord, have mercy" is the humble act of recognizing weakness and the desire for the compassionate presence that will restore what we have broken. The experience of God's mercy will enable us to be merciful to others.

This understanding of mercy lies behind the evolution of the Jesus Prayer that is so important among Eastern Orthodox Christians: "Lord Jesus Christ, Son of the living God, have mercy on me, a sinner." Supplications like these release deep psychological anxiety and open us to the restoration of a healthy relationship with God. That may lie behind the words in Luke's gospel about love of enemies—"Love your enemies, do good, and lend, expecting nothing in return. Your reward will be great, and you will be children of the Most High; for he is kind to the ungrateful and the wicked. Be merciful, just as your Father is merciful" (Luke 6:35–36).

When Abba Isaac speaks of "prayers," he is not referring to those articulated with words but of prayer as personal *movement* toward God. He speaks of prayers as actions we take to meet and become formed by the One who is present in the words we have been reciting from the Bible or articulating from the heart. By thus offering something to God, we let go of our attachment to "an earthly way of life" while still remaining in the world. We offer ourselves to God "with utter earnestness of heart." Our prayer is transformed from mere words to an experience of God's presence that evokes our desire to serve God with our whole being. In this way, ministry proceeds from intimacy with God.

Modern Christians usually think of prayer primarily as "intercessions," which are Abba Isaac's third type of prayer. We pray *for* something or someone. Abba Isaac reminds us, however, that our intercessions take place in the context of meditation on biblical texts, awareness of our failings, and our desire to "serve the Lord with utter earnestness of heart." Our prayers for other people and for the needs of the world flow from an earnest relationship with God, and in this way our pleas for the wellbeing of others and the whole world will emerge from our discernment of what God desires and not be limited solely to our perspective. Intercession also bonds us to those for whom we pray.

It is significant that Abba Isaac saves his most passionate words for his description of giving thanks. Thanksgiving is offered in "unspeakable ecstasies," both by the mind and the spirit. By remembering God's gifts to us in the past and the present, as well as "foreseeing what great things God has prepared for those who love him," we are led to a sense of gratitude that transcends words. This is more than a thank-you note to God. Such intense gratefulness can lead our spirits to discern God's eternal love for us and give thanks with "boundless joy." This is fire!

UNFINISHED PORTRAITS

As we have seen, these four forms of personal praying, combined with meditation on biblical texts (especially the life of Jesus) and participation in the sacramental life of the church, formed the environment of grace that sustained the lives of the earliest Christians. These aspects of personal prayer were built on a foundation of contemplative prayer and meditation. Our prayer today stands on the shoulders of this rich tradition that offers us both challenge and immense discernment and power for daily living. The challenge is to become who we already are.

Saint John of the Cross, a sixteenth-century monastic reformer, poet, and theologian, affirmed that although we are created in the image of God, we do not automatically live according to our true nature. We must gradually acquire and manifest the likeness of God in our manner of life through a lifelong process of openness to transformation. He called this process "the sketch of Christ being filled out in us." We are unfinished portraits. Prayer is the canvas on which the face of Christ becomes known through the features of our lives.

The second half of this book will introduce you to two disciplines for caring for your soul. If you are already familiar with meditation and contemplative prayer, perhaps this narrative will affirm and strengthen what you already practice. Each of these ascetic disciplines has many variations and is rooted in thousands of years of Christian spiritual formation and experience.

Chapter Four

Love

Prayer is not something we do. Prayer is someone we become, with God's grace. As we experience God in personal prayer we are also challenged to become an incarnation of that experience in our active lives. We are called to embody what we have begun to experience. The integration of contemplation and meditation with loving behavior is rooted in this truth. "A real man or woman of prayer," as Evelyn Underhill wrote, "should be a live wire, a link between God's grace and the world that needs it." Our personal prayer and our active engagement with society are expressions of two aspects of the same reality; they are linked together just as an electric wire connects energy from its source to the computer on which I am writing this book or the lamp on my desk.

Our primary mentor in learning about the integration of prayer and daily life is Jesus of Nazareth. His example will show that personal prayer is not a private or isolated sector of our lives, but a necessary part of everyday living. It is Jesus who showed us that prayer is the flow of the energy of God. It is not possible for us to understand or experience the essence of God on our own, although this does not mean that God is distant or uninvolved in our lives. We learn from Jesus that the Spirit of God flows out from God's essence, from the divine mystery, to reveal itself in time and space and in the heart of every human being. The flow of God's energy, which Jesus called the Spirit, became manifest in a unique way in Jesus of Nazareth. The life of Jesus was a constant flow of his life into the heart of God and of God's love into the heart of Jesus.

To understand this it may be helpful to imagine the heart as an inner landscape where we experience and respond to divine Love. Our experience in this landscape enables us to recognize that same inner landscape as it is expressed in the outward appearance of other people, the lilies of the field, and the birds of the air. The poet Gerard Manley Hopkins called this outward shining of an unseen reality an "inscape." When our heart recognizes and bonds with the "inscape" of a friend, child, widow, enemy, refugee, animal, flower, city skyline, or battlefield, it loses its sense of separation and experiences the attraction of shared existence and love.

In the same way, Jesus' heart became the source of all his words and actions. It was his consciousness and the source of his power and wisdom, a revelation of the love of God. This is what John the Evangelist means when he says that God is love. The flow of love between Jesus and God, whom he called Abba and Holy One, was the flow of the Spirit between them. This flow of God's energy is what we call prayer. Jesus made it very clear to those who were close to him that this prayer was the source of his life here on earth, and that this same life of prayer is possible for every person willing to accept it. Jesus did not experience his Abba as an "other"; he was vividly aware that his thoughts, desires, words, and actions were not separate from God, and his passionate desire was to lead others to this same shared relationship. This is the heart of human transformation—to take on the consciousness of Jesus. All human beings can come to this shared experience of God. My "inscape" is your "inscape." We become one in Christ.

It is the humanness of Jesus that makes it possible for us to take part in the same flow of prayer between ourselves and God that he experienced. Human transformation in the Christian tradition is the willingness in each one of us to take on the consciousness of Jesus through the gift of the Spirit. The image Jesus used for this taking on of another's consciousness is "dying to self." The beginning of our transformation is our willingness to let go of control of ourselves in order to release the flow of Christ's consciousness in us. This is what Jesus desired for every person in his lifetime here on earth. How did this take place in the life of Jesus?

JESUS' LIFE OF PRAYER

When I was Steward of the Episcopal House of Prayer, a contemplative retreat center on the grounds of Saint John's Benedictine Abbey in Minnesota, I was asked to help lead a two-week seminar on the essential role of contemplative prayer in congregations. People were coming from all over the country and I was getting stage fright. What did I know? In preparation for this retreat I decided to examine the life of Jesus and so I spent three months reading all four gospels through three times. I looked for patterns in the life of Jesus that would give me a picture of his life of prayer. Here is what I found.

The four gospels reveal a pattern in Jesus' life that was the source of his union with God and in turn gave birth to all that he did and said. That is why he could say, "Do you not believe that I am in the Father and the Father is in me? The words that I say to you I do not speak on my own; but the Father who dwells in me does his works. Believe me that I am in the Father and the Father is in me; but if you do not, then believe me because of the works themselves" (John 14:10–11). Here is the simple pattern of Jesus' life of prayer I discovered:

- ✍ quiet listening;
- ✍ faithful discernment;
- ✍ compassionate response.

Regardless of how busy or tired he was, Jesus always found time to listen to God, to the world around him, and to his inner self. This listening heart was what led and sometimes drove him into compassionate involvement in the lives of others. Jesus' life of prayer opened him to the vitality of God's energy and vision. He became what he sought. He loved what he saw. He transformed what he touched. He lived what he spoke.

All this took place in the context of his own religious community, where Jesus' mystical and personal relationship with God became integrated with social interaction and responsibility. He seemed to be saying, "The realm of God is within you and is lived all around you" (Luke 17:21). Mirrored in Jesus' life is the wisdom and challenge that prayer is at the same time a personal journey and an opportunity to transform society. Prayer and living must be in harmony with each other; they are the same reality.

What are the implications of Jesus' life of prayer for us? Is it more important to declare who Jesus is or to live as he lived? Jesus was less interested in what people said about him than in revealing God's presence in his life and inviting people to share that same experience. Entering into the life of Jesus of Nazareth does not come through theological reflection or debate about right belief or right behavior. It comes by experiencing the divine life that was present in him. That is his challenge to us. It becomes a reality in our lives when we take his life seriously and are open to his transformed presence.

Jesus was passionate about wanting those who were close to him not only to share his intimate relationship with God but also but to mirror forth God's words and power in their lives. That is why he said not only, "Abide in me as I abide in you," but also, "The one who believes in me will also do the works that I do and, in fact, will do greater works than these, because I am going to the Father" (John 15:4; 14:12). This is living by faith: placing our lives into the life of the risen Christ. By accepting him as our Way and by committing ourselves to that path we experience what is true and most fully alive. Our life becomes our prayer. We make Christ tangible in the world.

Being attentive to God in prayer does not eliminate the distractions and conflicts of life, nor the hard work and responsibilities we share with so many others, but it does put these experiences solidly within the perspective of our relationship with God. We sort them out by looking at the reality of God and respond to them as we are able to discern God's desires for the world. Our response becomes a compassionate and responsible activism wherein we are freed from self-interest through the clear, constant, and transforming experience of God. Contemplation and meditation make shared action with God possible. This was a constant desire in Jesus' life. He called those who were willing to follow him to a mutual vocation of compassion. The fullness of who we are will unfold in our emptiness and become manifest in our work. Just as the dawn cannot be rushed, so is the dawn of our fullness in God.

The energy within personal prayer and action flows in two directions. Action, as well as contemplation, is a context in which we meet God and become aware of God's desires for ourselves and for the world. Our active lives give a sense of integrity to our contemplative experience by preventing it from becoming self-centered and bringing it to life in our work and relationships. Contemplation in a world of action does not mean blending together two completely separate aspects of our lives. These two always work together even though we may emphasize one or the other at different times or even neglect one for the other. They are as inseparable as breathing in and breathing out in one harmonious rhythm that makes us fully alive.

LABOR AND PRAXIS

The desert mothers and fathers relied on Jesus' wisdom as the foundation of their understanding of prayer and work. They made a distinction between *labor* (physical work) and *praxis* (spiritual work). Physical labor contributes to God's creation and makes it possible to have a physical venue for our spiritual work; praxis is work directed toward a purely spiritual purpose. It includes bodily disciplines as well as an inner disposition or character that influences our whole being.

Labor and praxis are not in competition, nor should either be neglected in our lives. Instead they must be kept in balance, so that the listening and inner growth of praxis is integrated with the physical labors that make human life possible. This balance can remind us that our praxis should never be at someone else's expense, nor should our labor seek any benefits that go beyond our basic needs, physical or spiritual. This is the intent of monastic "poverty." Its source is gratitude and its fruit is generosity. Is it possible for you and me to have needs that are easily satisfied?

Labor, intertwined with praxis, becomes a process in which we learn to guide our will into harmony with God's will. As we are able, through praxis, to let go of our egocentricity and the desire to control our lives, our labor becomes dedicated to God's desires for the world.

Thus, labor may give us the opportunity to be supported by love as God's loving presence is embodied in our work.

The wisdom of the desert reminds us that when our daily labor is disconnected from daily spiritual practice, we tend to develop a passionate attachment to physical possessions and material security. This leads to greed, desire for power, and a denial of the spiritual dimension of life and work. The result of praxis should be openness to God and the world, not personal abundance; the primary purpose of labor is the welfare of the soul. When the two are integrated, labor becomes an opportunity to make the work accomplished both an offering to God and an offering of one's self and one's life to those around us. Thus to work is also to pray. Our work becomes filled with grace because it is an occasion on which God is with us as collaborator. That is how we become whole persons, and learn to experience an undivided life.

 Chapter Five

Soul

If prayer is a sacred conversation, when did the conversation begin? Who said the first prayer? If the meaning of the conversation is love, who are the lovers and whom do they love?

The first prayer is recorded in the Hebrew scriptures. The second chapter of Genesis declares, "Then the LORD God formed the human of dust from the earth, and breathed into the human's nostrils the breath of life; and the human became a living being" (Genesis 2:7, my translation). A human being is merely physical until it is empowered by divine energy, and only then does the human become a "living being." We are not complete until the body and its divine vitality are joined. The "living being," or soul, is a unity of the physical and psychic aspects of human life. The "living being," the soul, springs forth as a direct result of God's "breathing" the divine energy into the human being's nostrils. When God shares God's breath with each human being, the sacred "conversation" between that "living being" and God begins. God initiates each person's first prayer. This sharing of God's energy with each human being is the most profound declaration of the purpose of human life.

The Hebrew scriptures declare that a human being is not a corporeal substance that God then supplies with a soul (*nephesh*); rather, a human being is a living soul. The *essence* of a human being is her or his soul, and the soul encompasses and reflects every aspect of that person's life. "Soul" and "body" are not separate sectors of a person's life; together they constitute the *totality* of a living soul. The body does not "house" the soul. A human being is a living soul and the physical, emotional, psychic, rational, and spiritual aspects of each of our lives are reflected and embodied in the way we live and pray. It is the living soul that responds to God's initiative in prayer.

The sharing of God's breath with *adam*, the human being, shows that the meaning of that first prayer is love and it identifies the lovers. But how will love continue, and what will it look like? When Jesus was asked by the scribes, "Which commandment is the first of all?" he replied, "The first is, 'Hear O Israel: the Lord our God, the Lord is one; you shall love the Lord your God with all your heart, and with all your soul, and with all your mind, and with all your strength.' The second is this, 'You shall love your neighbor as yourself'" (Mark 12:28–31). In both instances he is quoting from the Hebrew scriptures, first from Deuteronomy and then from Leviticus, where the law forbids oppressing the neighbor—in this case the poor of Israel. Jesus is saying that we are created to love God with everything we are: our soul. But that is not all. Knowing we are loved by God, we are to love our neighbors in the same way that we care for our own sacred lives. We are a source of God's love for other people who, in turn, are called to love God and us. We are not separate; we are a unity of love.

This "first prayer" of Genesis gives us another gift, which is a vision of the abundance and sanctity of life. It identifies our true nature and gives us a way of looking at ourselves and the world. Prayer is the source of enlightened, compassionate, and responsible living.

The breath of God makes us a living soul, but it is not intended to be a one-time "mountaintop" experience. It will sustain our lives every day through a sharing of that same original energy. This is clearly the intent of Jesus when, after his resurrection, he appeared to his disciples in a locked room and breathed on them, saying, "Receive the Holy Spirit" (John 20:22). Jesus takes the initiative by breathing his life into those whom he loves, sharing the Spirit who will give them the "mind of Christ." It is a foretaste of authentic human life. This is why prayer is necessary—and the most fundamental way we care for our soul. If praying is caring for the soul, then it is caring for *everything* we are, not just the "religious" part of our lives. Prayer is essential for our whole human being.

Do you not know you are a temple of the Holy Spirit? You are a house of prayer.

STEWARDSHIP OF YOUR LIFE

Praying is caring for your soul. Without the awareness that we are created in the image of God and called to be partakers of the divine nature, we will lose sight of what it means to be human. For the dance to continue we must embrace our partner. When we separate ourselves from God we cast off our humanity and begin to live a lie. Yet God is present even in the lie, beckoning us in the midst of the things we do that separate us from God. In the words of Saint Augustine of Hippo, a fourth-century bishop and monk who found God later in life, "I was kept from Thee by those things, yet had they not been in Thee, they would not have been at all."

Silence is the birthplace of the listening and praise which daily restore our humanity by transforming our consciousness. No institution, technology, or human expertise will end human suffering, conflict, greed, war, injustice, and fear. Only transformed human beings will transform our world. We cannot foresee such transformation by ourselves, but must listen to God's voice and be open to God's vision. If we learn to recognize God's voice in contemplation and meditation, we will be able to hear that same voice in the midst of daily life. When we pay attention to God as the source of true insight, knowledge, and wisdom, our work, activities, decisions, and relationships will be transformed. We must be quiet in order to be human and learn to live into the likeness of God. The dance of life always begins with silence.

Today there are great battles waging between groups claiming to have unique access to "truth." Political, religious, and philosophical ideologies are engaged in struggles for people's hearts, influence, and allegiance; many of these battles lead to violence, physical torture, emotional abuse, and human and ecological catastrophe. Truth has become a weapon of control rather than a path to freedom. How can we know the truth? My own understanding of truth has changed over the years, mostly through my commitment to contemplative prayer. It has not been easy. I have learned that human certainty about knowledge or experience (which is truth from our human point of view) should be congruent with personal experience of God and what God desires for the world.

The origin of truth is God. Truth must bring forth life and liberation. My commitment is to recognize truth wherever I find it and to embody truth in my words and actions. This is impossible unless I rely on my experience of God in the silence of personal prayer and the wisdom of my faith community's experience of God. Sometimes I have been wrong. Sometimes the church has been wrong. But in our failures to recognize and live the truth, we learn to depend on God and seek the truth in silence. As the Syrian monk Isaac of Nineveh said, "Every person who delights in a multitude of words, even though he says admirable things, is empty within. If you love truth, be a lover of silence. Silence, like the sunlight, will illuminate you in God and will deliver you from the phantoms of ignorance. Silence will unite you to God."[6]

BARRIERS TO PRAYER

The busyness and high expectations of modern life lure us to into fragmentation. Allowing ourselves to be pulled in many directions at once leads us away from awareness of God. We become a creation of our own activity and begin to value only what we can define, control, or desire. Results rule! We can become so stranded in the wilderness of overactivity that we lose sight of the living beings all around us. The price we pay for giving in to this pressure for ever-greater productivity is a loss of clarity about life itself. We become unable to listen to anyone but ourselves, including God.

Our acceptance of this aspect of modern life is truly diabolical. The Greek roots of "diabolical," *dia* and *bolos*, mean to cast outward or become fragmented, losing direction and unity. This is the true nature of evil: it distracts, distorts, and fragments our lives. It hides what is real. Nothing is evil in itself: evil is the consequence of a distorted and broken way of seeing and living. The insidious power of evil or someone who perpetrates evil is that you may actually come to believe that what is being said or done can somehow be justified. Your ability to speak truth and demand and work for justice is diluted or muted by a false world of influence. How can we overcome fragmentation and regain and restore authentic vision and unity?

Jesus of Nazareth said, "If your eye is healthy [single], your whole body will be filled with light" (Matthew 6:22). We can restore wholeness in ourselves and then in society by slowing down the pace of our lives and taking time to listen. In an age that values constant motion and productivity, we need to develop the ability to relax. When we relax we can begin to be quiet and listen. We need solitude, stillness, openness, and silence to balance the necessary activities of life. John the Baptist told the curious crowds that came to see him at the Jordan River, "Among you stands one whom you do not know" (John 1:26). Like them, we need to be quiet in order to hear what lies within the noise and hyperactivity that so often surrounds us. The stillness will help us release our control of life and begin to become aware of what is true and fundamental. As we listen, we experience God's presence. Gradually, we will stop fearing the loss of control over ourselves and the personal environment we have worked so hard to create and maintain. This makes room for experience of God's love and the restoration of our trust in life. Life will become both the *symbol* and the venue of God's reliable presence and power.

Silence is the womb of union with God. Silence is like entering a desert that invites us to let go of things that distract us from God. Brother Roger, who founded an ecumenical monastic community in Taizé, France, writes, "When I chose the village of Taizé in 1940, I was alone. The silence of the desert strengthens the encounter with God. Man alone with himself is sensitive to a presence within him."[7] It is our path from fragmentation to wholeness. "In everyone there is a zone of solitude that no human intimacy can fill: it is there that God encounters us," he continues, reminding us that silence creates the space for our intellect and our heart to become one. It is from the unity of mind and heart that our will and action become a life of prayer. Our lack of vision and distorted values arise from the separation of mind and heart.

"In the morning place your intellect in your heart and remain all day in the company of God." This ancient prayer from the desert elders reminds us that human beings are *liturgical* beings. Our *lives* are meant to become prayer. When we allow God's spirit to bind our fragmented lives together, we become a living soul again. The ancient prayer ends saying, "By your love, bind my soul," exhorting the Spirit to reform our many moods, dissipated energies, and fragmented vision into a single and whole soul. Only then can our entire life be prayer. We become the celebrants of a daily liturgy that gives glory to God and new life to others.

FOR ALL

It is true that contemplation and meditation are *esoteric* practices. Esoteric refers to an inner dimension of life that cannot be seen and that lies, in mystery, beyond our grasp. Conventional wisdom concludes that anything esoteric is reserved for a small minority of persons whose lives focus inward and away from the mainstream of society. In this context contemplation and meditation are tolerated for the few, but are generally believed to have little to do with "real life." They are judged to have little practical value in a society with high expectations for tangible results. In today's world, results rule—so contemplative prayer and meditation are perceived as benign options but nothing more.

As we have seen, this is misguided because contemplative prayer and meditation are not for the "advanced" or elite, but for all. They lead to an awareness of the sanctity of creation and all living beings. This way of seeing life is the source of responsible living and compassionate relationships. Yet you and I can be the greatest obstacles to this vision. It is easy to live on the surface of life and become attached to our material needs and pleasures. When Jesus said, "You cannot serve God and wealth" (Matthew 6:24), he was not condemning material possessions but pointing to the danger of making worldly things and the power we need to protect them the center of our lives. This attachment can frame our entire vision of life. When we are devoted solely to personal needs and desires, even momentarily, our world becomes a world of "me" and "everything else." When Jesus tells us to store up treasure not on earth but in heaven, "for where your treasure is, there your heart will be also" (Matthew 6:21), "heaven" is not a future reality, but a transformed state of affairs in our lives right now. How do we find this authentic "treasure"? Jesus continues, "The eye is the lamp of the body. So, if your eye is healthy, your whole body will be full of light; but if your eye is unhealthy, your whole body will be full of darkness. If then the light in you is darkness, how great is the darkness!" (Matthew 6:22–23). Meditation and contemplation are the "eyes" that will change our consciousness.

Although I am not a psychologist nor a neurologist, I have learned a few things about consciousness from my life experience and the wisdom of my mentors. Consciousness has at least three dimensions. Being "conscious" is a state of being physically and neurologically awake, and it also means being aware of what is happening within and all around us. A third dimension, called the "subconscious," usually refers to an intuitive awareness of something that is not perceived directly, but all three dimensions are ways that we get in touch with reality. Consciousness is the window or lens through which each of us perceives our interior and exterior life—it is the way we "see life." It shapes our knowledge, relationships, and actions; it will influence the development of our core values. Consciousness is an essential aspect of our life with God, other persons, our work, families, society, and creation. This "vision" of life shapes our judgments, decisions, and behavior. Therefore our consciousness is a fundamental and practical part of getting things done and doing them well.

Together the four canonical gospels present a portrait of the "consciousness" of Jesus. Jesus taught that authentic knowledge of God flows from experience of and union with God. Once we know God through our personal experience, we can recognize God's presence and wisdom everywhere in life. This is what Jesus meant when he said, "If you know me, you will know my Father also. From now on you do know him and have seen him" (John 14:7). People who listened to Jesus' teaching experienced his consciousness of God and saw it as the source of his authority: "Now when Jesus had finished saying these things, the crowds were astounded at his teaching, for he taught them as one having authority, and not as their scribes" (Matthew 7:28–29).

But how does our consciousness come to reflect the way God sees the world? Is this a pious fantasy? I know that I have said, "The way I see it . . . " many, many times in my life. But is the way *I* see "it" the way "it" really is? I know that my own point of view directs my actions. My temptation is to assume that my vision of a situation is the right one for choosing a course of action, whereas meditation and contemplative prayer offer a wider perspective through teaching me the discipline of listening to Someone besides myself. A listening heart is the link to seeing as God sees.

Contemplative prayer and meditation are disciplines in the art of listening with the ear of the heart and seeing with eyes of love. They are the womb of *sacred consciousness.* They link the head with the heart and join work to the spiritual dimension of life. They are simple, yet their effects can be profound. Although these forms of praying may seem passive, they are essential parts of getting things done and doing them well. They are concerned with the source and motives of our actions. For Christians this means having "the mind of Christ" (1 Corinthians 2:16). The words belong to Saint Paul, who was speaking out of his conversion on the road to Damascus. His consciousness was changed from that of a person who persecuted the followers of Jesus to one who saw Jesus in a totally new light. While staying in a house in Damascus, "something like scales fell from his eyes" (Acts 9:18) and he received a totally new way of seeing the world and those around him. Henri Nouwen reminds us that this is an audacious challenge: "Indeed, we are called to know what Jesus knew and do what Jesus did. Do we really want that, or do we prefer to keep Jesus at arms' length?"

Contemplation and meditation also help us discern what we are becoming in the midst of our activity. They provide an opportunity to collaborate with God in the formation of our consciousness and offer a way of sacred listening and seeing before we leap into action. Vaclav Havel, the former president of the Czech Republic, affirms this challenge in the context of current world affairs:

> Consciousness precedes being, and not the other way around, as the Marxists claim. For this reason, the salvation of this human world lies nowhere else than in the human heart, in the human power to reflect, in human meekness and in human responsibility. Without a global revolution in the sphere of human consciousness, nothing will change in the sphere of our being as humans, and the catastrophe toward which this world is headed—be it ecological, social, demographic, or a general breakdown of civilization— will be unavoidable.[8]

Modern culture seems committed to forms of materialism that are blind to the sanctity of people and of natural resources. Vaclav Havel reminds us that we do this at our peril. If we do not pay attention to the spiritual dimension of life in our daily life of prayer, our lives will continue to be incomplete and filled with anxiety. The twenty-first century began with great hopes for meeting the challenges that face humanity, but now we seem hopelessly enmeshed in war, terrorism, continuing hunger, and poverty, as well as in a struggle for hegemony between cultures, nations, and religious traditions. We are impatient and want to fix it all ourselves as quickly as possible. Lack of civility in public life and unwillingness to listen to each other make reconciliation difficult. Without meditation and contemplation, our hearts will have little room for listening to God. Vaclav Havel reminds us that we need a change of consciousness—a change in the way we see each other and the world. Without attention to our inner life, what will life become? As Havel stresses, prayer and the quality of public life are directly connected.

Several years ago I saw Vaclav Havel's principle in action. I was asked to speak to a group of community leaders in Minneapolis–St. Paul on the topic, "How can we bring God into the life of the city?" The daunting task of speaking to city services employees, healthcare professionals, politicians, educators, utilities managers, park managers, religious leaders, and directors of museums and programs for the arts forced me to think about city life in a new way. Then it hit me! Our task is not to try to *apply* God or the spiritual dimensions of life to the city, but to discern how God is *already present* in the city. The spiritual dimension already dwells in every aspect of the city, represented by the civic leaders in the boardroom that morning. When all these ordinary parts of city life are seen as more than buildings, parks, hospitals, transportation grids, schools, services, and political infrastructure, they teach us new possibilities in the stewardship of city life. They can form a tapestry that will enhance the way life is lived in the city and change the relationships between all sectors of city life and human relationships in the city. When the spiritual, or sacred, dimension is discerned in each sector or service, it takes on a new value and changes all the relationships around it, including the people of the city. This is a form of *conversation* between civic leaders and the presence of God in their areas of responsibility. Their jobs are more than jobs; the resources of the city are more than resources. Here is Havel's crucial connection between the quality of spiritual life and civic life. Without prayerful conversation, the spiritual presence within city life will remain hidden or seen as separate from its "secular" sectors. Unless individual civic leaders listen to God in their own lives, how will they be able to discern God's voice and presence in their cities and towns?

Architect Christopher Alexander is saying something similar when he speaks of a "quality without a name" in his book *The Timeless Way of Building*. He points out the limitations of words when they are used to describe the inward or spiritual dimension of life, particularly as it relates to buildings: "All things and people and places which have the quality without a name, reach into the realm of the eternal." Perhaps this is what Jesus of Nazareth meant when he said, "The realm of God is within you" (Luke 17:21). Alexander is convinced that we go back and forth between our awareness of this "quality without a name" and our usual way of being, where "inner contradictions rule." When a person, place, or thing is free from inner contradictions, it is part of the eternal and stands outside of time. Perhaps this is what Jesus had in mind when he said, "If your eye is healthy [single], your whole body will be filled with light." What gives something or someone this spiritual and numinous quality? What makes an encounter with an object or person lead us beyond itself? The early followers of the Way believed that God was present in an ordinary human life and was to be met there. The Christian experience of *incarnation* is that the "quality without a name" (what we call "God") lies within the ordinary, earthy, and natural created world.

Perhaps our inability to perceive God's presence in the ordinary and our resistance to the idea is caused by these "inner contradictions." Our desire to define and control the world around us contradicts the freedom of God's presence in us and our world. We contradict the ordinariness of the divine presence in ordinary things by declaring that the human realm must be totally *separate* from God. We name creation "the natural world" and convince ourselves that it is *unnatural* for God to be present in human life, in other living beings, places, and things.

"We have a habit of thinking that the deepest insights, the most mystical, and spiritual insights," writes Alexander, "are somehow less ordinary than most things—that they are *extraordinary*." He feels that these perceptions are shallow and that the opposite is true: what we think of as mysterious and wonderful, as "mystical," are in fact the most ordinary things of all. "It is because they are so ordinary, indeed, that they strike to the core."[9]

Contemplative experience takes place whenever we are struck to the core, whether we are in silent reflection or scientific research. Yet in today's society we value many things and activities that distract us from the "quality without a name." We seem to prefer the place where "inner contradictions" rule. In the midst of our necessary activities and responsibilities we all need times and places where we can be led beyond the words and boundaries of our self-created worlds. Then we are surrounded by hints of the presence of the One who is without a name. God is hidden everywhere—in plain view.

When I lived among Athabaskan Indians in Alaska, I traveled by dog team during the long and cold winters. I used my team to haul wood and ice and to travel to other villages to assist in the life of small congregations. "Driving" dogs means working with them and traveling slow enough to notice simple gifts, like mouse tracks in the snow, glistening ice crystals on spruce needles, the sound of wind, and the play of light, especially at dawn and dusk. I remember the advent of snowmobiles and the advantages that speed offered for efficiency of work and travel. But the noise and speed of rapid travel overpowered so many of the little things of life. Although my dog team required a lot of work to feed and care for them, they never ran out of gas or broke down. I used my snowmobile and was grateful for its convenience, but it changed my relationship with the world around me and I did my best to balance the two.

I miss my dog team now and in the midst of travel by car, bus, train, and airplane I still try to notice the little things of life. I walk as often as I can. When I sit on benches, café stools, and airport lounge seats, I take the time to notice who and what is around me. I still encounter the little things, along with some delightful surprises. It sounds too simple, too unsophisticated. It is tempting to spend the time reading, watching the ubiquitous television monitors, listening to canned music, or covering my ears with headphones. There are little things everywhere, both in forest and in city, with meaning and mystery in all of them.

Mahatma Gandhi said, "My life is my message." Contemplation and meditation are not simply prayerful behaviors. Each activity is also an exterior and interior *place*, like the isolated cells of the desert mothers and fathers. They wait for us, reminding us of who we are and, like a sunrise, giving light to each new day. There is nothing you or I can do to rush a sunrise. Hard as it is, we must be patient in prayer, waiting day after day for the presence of the Holy One.

Chapter Six

Discipline

In the Christian tradition there are two fundamental disciplines that guide each person's desire for experience of God: contemplation and meditation. These disciplines were the foundation of early Christian prayer that I described in previous chapters and offer the same reliable foundation for our lives of prayer today. Saint Benedict of Nursia, the sixth-century father of Benedictine monastic life, exhorted his monks to live "a disciplined life." The Latin words he used referred to an intentional "manner" or pattern of life that was freely chosen. Similarly, meditation and contemplation may be called disciplines or "patterns" of prayer. In the western Christian tradition *meditation* usually refers to a focus of attention on something that engages our mind and bodily senses, while *contemplation* means experiencing God's presence by letting go of conscious thought and sense experience. (In eastern Christianity as well as in the religions of the East, especially Buddhism, the opposite is true.) Although each discipline has unique features, both lead us to authentic experience of God's presence.

Meditation is known as the *kataphatic* way, a Greek word that illustrates the fundamental meaning and purpose of meditation. The prefix *kata* means "toward" or "in relation to"; and *phatic* (from *phasis*) refers to "saying" or "asserting" something. Thus the kataphatic way affirms that God may be experienced by using the mind and the body; in other words, it affirms what our senses, our imagination, and our reason perceive in prayer. Meditation is a pattern of prayer that discovers God's presence within nature, art, sacred scriptures, music, symbols, and various forms of liturgy. Meditation is a prayer of focus and intention, although the "result" of our specific intention is usually beyond our control. A walk in the woods or a city park may bring an unexpected insight that is felt in the heart, in addition to our visual perception of the beauty of a sunrise making dark leaves shine or backlighting a city skyline. Our feeble attempts to define what God is like are eclipsed by the wonder of God's presence in creation. A more disciplined form of meditation is *lectio divina,* where a passage from the Bible is read several times and we use the silence in between each reading to reflect on the meaning of the passage and its implication for daily living.

Contemplation is the *apophatic* way of personal prayer. The Greek prefix *apo* signifies "away from" and so *apophasis* means literally "saying away." Thus the apophatic way leads us away from saying or asserting anything definite about God; it is a kind of "unknowing." Rather than affirming what our mind and our senses tell us about God, as we do in meditation, in contemplation, we let go of words, mental activity, concepts, images, and metaphors, and all theology about God. We make room for God's presence by relinquishing not only the images of God that are most familiar to us through our thoughts and senses, but our desire for God as well. The apophatic way looks inward; it relies on awareness and openness to God's initiative. It emphasizes "unknowing," waiting, and vulnerability. It is prayer without boundaries and is content with simply being present in silence. In response to Jesus' call for personal transformation, contemplative prayer is a grace-filled attentiveness to God that initiates and sustains a change of consciousness leading to deepening love of God and neighbor.

This understanding of contemplative prayer is based on an awareness that Christian contemplation is grounded in the Bible and two thousand years of Christian tradition. It embraces a variety of practices that sustain our ability to "pray always," as Saint Paul exhorts. One example of apophatic prayer is the form of "centering prayer" taught by Father Thomas Keating, a Cistercian Roman Catholic monk. In centering prayer a person finds a quiet place and brings herself or himself into God's presence with a short prayer and then sits in silence for at least twenty minutes. A short prayer of thanksgiving brings the silence to a close.

The spirituality of most people is a combination of the apophatic and the kataphatic, the journey inward and the journey outward. Both paths enable us to experience an intimacy with God that will be the source of our compassionate engagement with the needs of the world. Meditation and contemplation are not competitors; both patterns of prayer offer different, yet complementary, ways of becoming aware of the mystical dimension of God's presence. Contemplation embraces the transcendence or "otherness" of God and meditation focuses on the immanence or "closeness" of God. Both are necessary to balance our experiences of God, even though most people feel more at home in one or the other.

Furthermore, some dimensions of each discipline are present in the other. Different people will be attracted to contemplation or meditation for a variety of reasons, such as personality type, a need for either a flexible or a more rigid discipline, artistic ability, love of thinking, desire for quiet, and many other factors. We should try to experience both contemplation and meditation for a reasonable period of time and discern which is best for our practice. As we shall see, meditation often leads toward contemplative experience of God. The fact that meditation and contemplation are seen as complementary within the Christian tradition of mysticism is a bold statement about the limitlessness of God's presence and the variety of ways we may experience that presence.

Many people use a variety of contemplative techniques for therapy, personal improvement, or just relaxation after a hectic day. There is nothing wrong with these practices. But Christian contemplation and meditation have no other goal than simply being with God and letting go of our needs, in trust. We do not always succeed, but that is our desire. We do not deny that "simply being with God" will influence our lives in a variety of ways. But ultimately we seek contemplative experience without personal expectations or controls. In this way, Christian contemplative experience is not better than other practices; it is simply *different*.

WE SHALL ALL BE CHANGED

Saint Paul wrote to the Corinthians about the possibility of radical change in Christ: "If anyone is in Christ, there is a new creation: everything old has passed away; see, everything has become new!" (2 Corinthians 5:17). Each person moves along her or his path to transformation in a unique way, although many aspects of the journey are shared in common. We need guidance and inspiration from mentors and teachers, but it is not wise to compare our progress with the maturity or wisdom of others. We walk this path together and are always beginners.

After Abba Arsenius had spent years in solitary prayer, his wisdom was sought by many disciples. One day they overheard him praying, "O God, do not leave me. I have done nothing good in your sight, but according to your goodness, let me now make a beginning of good." This is not an easy lesson. The desert mothers and fathers attracted visitors and disciples because their lives were congruent with their words. The maturity of their experience of God was tangible and contagious: people saw something in their lives that they desired for themselves. The desert elders' commitment to a substantive discipline of prayer and their openness to the movement of God's Spirit enabled them to mature in their life with God and embody a new and rich level of human consciousness. Yes, they had matured. They were experiencing a dimension of human life and of God that was different from other people. Yet they knew themselves well enough to realize they were not better than anyone else. For example, Abba Anthony had the humbling experience of learning that "there was one who was his equal in the city. He was a doctor by profession and whatever he had beyond his needs he gave to the poor, and every day he sang the Sanctus with the angels."

Each person lives a unique life. Some persons are called to the monastic vocation that intentionally devotes more time to prayer, study, and spiritual formation. All Christian lives are enriched by this monastic manner of life because it is a living reminder of every person's call to prayer and transformation. Monasticism offers us guidance and inspiration as we seek God in the lives we have chosen. In his commentary on the letter to the Hebrews, John Chrysostom described monastic life as a mirror for the vocation of all Christians: "When Christ orders us to follow the narrow path, he addresses himself to all persons. The monk and the lay person must attain the same heights." Realistically, we may not experience the same consciousness of God as a monk, hermit, or solitary, but Paul's exhortation to "imitate Christ" is the same.

All Christians share the same invitation to human transformation in Christ, even though the outcome of transformation will be different in every case. We will mature in Christ in different ways. Our goal is not "advancement" in the life of prayer, but faithfulness to the movement of God's Spirit in our lives. Transformation in the Christian tradition requires genuine desire and effort. That is something we all share. The rest is in God's loving hands, and that is the joy of the lure of divine love.

When we commit our lives to God in prayer we *will* experience change and mature, but it is not our doing. We may not even be aware of what is taking place in us, and we are not in control. God is drawing us to an ever-new way of seeing and living. We should avoid becoming attached to what is taking place in us and avoid comparing ourselves to anyone else. What we *are* is always a gift, and we should resist thinking of ourselves as more advanced or mature than someone else. At the same time, we can share what we have become and learned with others, not because we feel superior, but because we are aware that we walk the same path together and need each other's help. The teacher's gift is the presence and wisdom of God; the gift given by the student to the teacher is the opportunity to be a vessel of God's grace. Abba Pachomius believed that there is no greater vision than that of the presence of the living God in the life of a human being. We can rejoice in each person's life, knowing that we are all called to be a blessing.

THE UNIQUENESS OF CHRISTIAN PRAYER

Every human being is called to experience God, and contemplation and meditation are part of almost all religious traditions. Yet each tradition, while sharing basic similarities regarding the purpose and practice of contemplative experience, has its unique understanding and disciplines. These differences reflect the diversity of human cultures and creativity as well as the limitlessness of God's intercourse with human beings. Although very different and sometimes impossible to reconcile, each tradition can enlighten the others. Authentic experience of God is not the possession of any single religious tradition.

Then what is unique about *Christian* contemplative experience? It is important to understand that uniqueness does not imply exclusivity. We can be committed to and desire to share our unique experience of God without insisting that it is the only path to life with God. In fact, our Christian experience can be enlightened by God's presence in the wisdom and practice of other traditions.

It has been difficult for me to accept this truth. Like many people, I have enjoyed my study of other religious traditions, but have usually looked at them through the lenses of my Christian belief and experience. So I considered myself "accepting" of other religions—which meant that rather than being prejudiced, I was only patronizing! My moment of truth came during my doctoral studies in religious education at New York University, where I found myself in the midst of students from Judaism, Islam, Hinduism, the Moonies, Buddhism, Shinto, and New Age beliefs. It was a delightful experience of the whole range of humankind's experience of God. My best friend during this two-year period was a Buddhist priest from Korea. We stayed up all night in his apartment celebrating the Buddha's birthday with traditional Korean food, he visited my family on Long Island, and we had many late-night discussions. I was criticized by some Christian friends for welcoming him in my home and exposing my children to his influence.

But it was not until I studied with a disciple of Swami Vivekananda, a Hindu guru, that my moment of truth arrived. His teaching was filled with wisdom and his boundaries for seeking truth were transparent, even though some of it seemed foreign to me. One night in the

NYU library, as I summarized what I was learning from him, I went into a state of panic. "What if he is right?" Suddenly it seemed my Christian belief and experience was being challenged—how could Christianity and Hinduism both be "right"? I was afraid I would have to choose between the two traditions in order to find the truth. Finally, after several weeks of struggle, the New Testament came to my rescue. In both his letter to the Romans and his first letter to the Corinthians, Saint Paul says that God has been revealing God's self since the beginning of human life, and the ways in which God may be known are virtually limitless. Not everyone was able to discern that wisdom, but God was always at work.

Paul helped me realize the distinction between *uniqueness* and *exclusivity*. He is very firm in his statements about the uniqueness of the identity of Jesus Christ and of what he makes possible for human life, but the Christian tradition does not exhaust all there is to say and experience of the wisdom and power of God. I was not only relieved, I was liberated! This did not mean I could have my cake and eat it, too—I was not free to craft my personal religious way from a variety of sources. I was relieved and liberated because I could accept the integrity of my own Christian path and the integrity of the Swami's path as well. We do not agree on everything, but neither tradition may claim sole access to the Truth or claim to be the only venue for God's presence in the universe. I am unapologetically Christian to the roots of my being, but my Christian path has been and continues to be enlightened and strengthened by other religious traditions. That is a gift of God.

The primary uniqueness of Christian contemplative life is its focus on Jesus of Nazareth and the risen Christ. In Christian experience it is Jesus who reveals and leads us to the Holy One, the reality of God. Therefore, most of our desires to experience God and manifest God's presence in our lives are focused on and led by our contemplation of the life, death, resurrection, and ascension of Jesus as presented in the gospels. Our contemplation and meditation are Christ-centered. Our consciousness of God, of ourselves, and of our world is fully developed as we seek oneness with God in Christ. Jesus Christ is the window through which we look into the heart of God, where we experience love and are freed and empowered to love our neighbors.

The other unique aspect of Christian contemplative experience is our understanding of *incarnation*. God is revealed to us both in creation and in Jesus Christ. At the same time, Jesus himself realized that we too are called to reveal God in the world through being united with God in contemplation and meditation. This does not mean we will lose our humanity in God, or become God. Our union with God is a mystery, just as the life, death, and resurrection of Jesus are filled with mystery. The important thing is to live into the mystery rather than try to explain it.

The next two chapters will discuss meditation and contemplation in more detail and provide guidance and examples for each discipline.

Chapter Seven

Meditation

The word "meditation" is related to the Latin phrase *sto in medio,* meaning "I stand in the center." Meditation is thus a path into the center of life. It is any form of prayer in which we use our senses and our understanding to focus on God's intimate presence within us and all around us. So someone learning to meditate will have many options, including words, Bible passages, prayers, chants, or visual images — from the simple burning of a candle to gazing on a sacred icon or painting. These are only a few of the options that may help us discern God's presence and desires for us and the world.

While contemplation seeks God by temporarily *turning away* from what is revealed by our senses and our imaginations, meditation seeks God *in them.* It helps us to discover God's presence in everything around us. Every word of scripture, every flower, every work of art, every living creature, every heavenly body has a part in God's desires for the life of the world. In meditation we learn about and experience God within created things because their inner dimension shares the energies of the God who made them. I know this is true every time I look through the eyepiece of my telescope, photograph a wildflower with my digital camera, read and reflect on a passage from the Bible, sit in the presence of an icon, or reflect on a poem by Rumi or Mary Oliver.

But you do not have to be an amateur astronomer or live on five acres in a hemlock forest to be aware of God's presence. One method is to use the "spaces" in between the tasks you have to do at home or at work. These spaces do not have to be long periods of time. Rather than multitasking, take a moment to look at a picture on the wall or a calendar on your desk that has a word of wisdom or prayer. You may be surprised at what happens within you during this breathing space between tasks.

Although I live in a rural area now, I was born in New York City and still feel a deep kinship with life in the city whenever I go there to visit or teach. It takes six hours by bus from my hemlock forest to Manhattan. As I set off from Port Authority Bus Terminal, I wait on each street corner for the "walk" sign to be illuminated, even though I could rush across with the crowds. It is very frustrating just to stand there with humanity rushing past and coming toward me, but standing and waiting provides an opportunity to meditate. I have learned that as I stand, I begin to notice individual people, trees (the few that I can see), and details on buildings around me that are treasures supported by the cement floor of the city. This is not a "mountaintop" experience, but by slowing down and allowing myself more time, I am less caught up in the rush of city life that so many people complain is inhuman.

Another possibility is to allow yourself more time for mundane chores, like shopping for groceries. My son Matthew is an assistant to an ambassador in Washington, D.C., and after a particularly busy day he takes time at his favorite market to look carefully at the produce, fruit, meat, and seafood, and to talk to the employees. He gets to know them and finds himself becoming more grateful for the variety of foods—the colors, the smells, the shapes, and the possibilities for a good meal. How many times have you been somewhere and, like Jacob encountering angels ascending and descending on a ladder from heaven, thought, "Surely the LORD is in this place—and I did not know it!" (Genesis 28:16).

City parks and greenbelts provide opportunities for prayer because they offer a place apart where you can relax from the usual rhythms and responsibilities of each day. These green spaces can be a place for listening and mindfulness that help take you "beyond" what is pressing in on you at work or at home and keep you from taking yourself too seriously. Even window boxes bring verdancy and color to a "sit-and-stare" moment looking out the window.

Museums of all kinds can be places of prayer. Prayer is a conversation and most often the language we use is rational. Museums, however, engage us with images that help us to a more complete experience of life, including its sacred dimension. A science museum will show us life in all its organic complexity and interdependence; art museums allow us to transcend our own limited point of view and see life through the creativity of other persons. This creativity may also inspire us to search for our own talents and challenge us to find innovative ways of discovering God's presence. Art helps us be in conversation with God without relying on our usual certainties.

In the city there are also hundreds of opportunities to visit mosques, synagogues, and Christian churches. These are places set aside as "sacred" spaces and we can visit them on lunch breaks or in the evening or early morning; we can attend special concerts, lectures, and regular services in them. But their primary purpose is not to say, "Here is God," but to help us experience God wherever we go. Visiting the sacred spaces of a variety of religious traditions can become a prayer of "awareness" that will draw us into the variety of ways God becomes present in human lives and will open our eyes to the ways other traditions experience God's intimacy and respond to God's love.

FURTHER SUGGESTIONS FOR MEDITATION

Many Christian monastic communities follow a rhythm of prayer and meditation that enables the brothers and sisters to remain in the company of God in the midst of other important activities in each day. This practice is called praying the monastic hours and usually includes pausing for short services of prayer and meditation from four to seven times a day. Here are two very simple alternatives, inspired by the monastic offices, for the beginning and end of each day. (You may also develop your own "book of hours" based on your work schedule and lifestyle.) Praying the morning and evening "hours" will place you in God's presence at the beginning and ending of each day and remind you that you are loved unconditionally. When you begin each day knowing you are loved, you will eventually develop an attitude of gratefulness that will influence every aspect of your daily relationships and tasks. When you end each day in the awareness of God's love then you will be able offer that day as a gift, aware of its accomplishments and pleasures as well as its failures or missed opportunities. Offering yourself to God at the end of the day will help you accept yourself, remind you of the sanctity of your life, and help you rely on God for newness of life.

Matins

Soon after waking and rising, let your body express a sense of gratefulness for the new day and an openness to God's presence. (I love to raise my arms toward the ceiling, open my hands, then kneel and place my forehead on the floor.) You may want to say this ancient prayer from the Psalms:

O Holy One, open my lips,
that my mouth may declare your praise.

Then read a short passage from the Bible, either silently or out loud, and reflect on it for one or two minutes. There are many ways to choose scripture passages, ranging from the use of a Bible lectionary with set readings for each day, which are found in the worship books of most denominations, to reading one book of the Bible in full, such as Genesis, a prophet such as Amos or Jeremiah, or one of the gospels.

For more specific suggestions for finding biblical passages, see *Too Deep for Words* by Thelma Hall or Norvene Vest's *No Moment Too Small: Rhythms of Silence, Prayer, and Holy Reading.* For passages from a variety of world religious traditions, see *God Makes the Rivers to Flow: Passages for Meditation* by Eknath Easwaran. You may recite a psalm as your primary scripture passage or include it just before another passage from the Bible or other sacred text. *Psalms for Praying: An Invitation to Wholeness* is a meditative version of the biblical Psalms by Nan C. Merrill, and a new translation that retains the poetic beauty of the original Hebrew is Lynn Bauman's *Ancient Songs Sung Anew: The Psalms as Poetry.*

Read the passage again, pause briefly, and bring your morning hour to a close with one of these ancient prayers:

Bind my head and my heart in you, Holy One,
and may I remain in your company this day.

The grace of Jesus Christ, the love of God,
and the companionship of the Holy Spirit
be with me in each moment of this day.

May the strength of God guide me this day,
    and may God's power preserve me.
May the wisdom of God instruct me,
    and the eye of God watch over me.
May the ear of God hear me,
    and the word of God give sweetness
    to my speech.
May the hand of God defend me,
    and may I follow the way of God.

You may also want to carry the scripture passage you chose with you throughout the day and let it speak to you.

Vespers
After supper or before getting ready for bed, spend a short period of time in silence. Then begin Vespers with this prayer adapted from the Psalms:

O God, come to my assistance,
O Holy One, make haste to help me.

Then, as you did in the morning, choose a short passage from the Bible and reflect on it for one or two minutes. Read the passage again, pause briefly, and bring your evening hour to a close with this ancient prayer:

Into your hands, O God, I entrust my spirit.

You will find, in time, that being aware of God's presence and commending your life to God first thing in the morning and again in the evening will become a strong foundation for each day, regardless of what the day brings into your life. The power of personal prayer is that it will keep you rooted and grounded in God rather than yourself.

Meleté

Meleté, pronounced *mell-eh-tay*, is the practice of repeating a verse, phrase, or short passage throughout the day. It is an ancient Christian monastic discipline. This simple practice, silently or aloud at different times during the day, can help you remain centered in God's presence in the midst of the distractions and responsibilities that consume your time and energies every day.

In the morning choose your verse, phrase, or passage. Memorize it or write it on a small slip of paper. You may want to have a small notepad to use just for this practice. During the day repeat it from memory or read it whenever you have the desire or opportunity. Try not to analyze the verse or passage. Let it enter your consciousness without expectations. At the end of the day say or read it one more time and spend a short period of silence resting in its wisdom before you let it go. You can use words or passages from the Bible or some other trusted prayer resource of quotations from the riches of Christian teaching and tradition. Two websites that will email you short quotations for each day of the week are found at www.HenriNouwen.org and www.gratefulness.org

Mindfulness

Mindfulness is a natural form of prayer that is often overlooked. It is part of our standard equipment but needs to be cultivated. Mindfulness is the simple act of being present to one thing at a time. It is living in the present moment.

The focus of mindfulness may be on a single task or activity. In that case, your attention and energy will be directed to what you are doing in the moment, even if it is mundane or boring. Modern society values multitasking and most institutions reward people who are able to accomplish more than one thing at a time. In some cases multitasking is essential and may save lives, but recent psychological studies have shown that it actually results in less efficiency and produces unnoticed stress. Mindfulness will help you focus on the task at hand and center your physical, psychological, and spiritual energies. It will help you see and connect with the task and its energy and then be able to move on to the next task with the unique focus it deserves. A pattern of mindfulness will give value to each activity and help you avoid taking your work for granted. Life is more than just getting things done. What are you becoming as you work? This prayerful attention will bring a spiritual dimension to your work.

Mindfulness is also being aware of little and large things all around you. It will help you notice things you can easily miss if you move too rapidly through each day. Mindfulness is a demeanor of attentive openness and wonder that gives birth to gratefulness. It is looking at one thing, place, or person at a time, without analysis or judgment. If you see a rose, just look at the rose. Avoid thoughts like, "It's more graceful than the one next to it," or "Those petals are turning brown." If, at sunset, you look out across a campus, over a lake or field, or down a busy city street, let the moment be itself. Rather than thinking, "That is so beautiful," let the beauty embrace you silently. Mindfulness lets you encounter the naked reality of each object and experience its unique energy.

The prayer of mindfulness will transform your relationships by helping you honor the presence of another person. If you are in conversation with another person, for example, mindfulness will help you avoid crafting your response before she or he has finished. Approaching other persons without positive or negative judgment is a first step toward discerning the common good. It is a form of prayer.

In time, you will discover that mindfulness helps you become more aware of life. Without ignoring things you must get done, mindfulness will slow you down so you will not miss the uniqueness of each day. This is true when your days bring difficult tasks, disappointments, conflicts, pain, or awareness of the pain and needs of others. It takes time to cultivate the prayer of mindfulness.

Mindfulness is also the willingness to be vulnerable, to be acted upon. It is your desire to direct your whole being toward experience of life in a naked and mutual seeing. Mindfulness will help you discern that life is a gift of God, even with its difficulties. It will help you see beyond the horizons of life that you or others have determined for you, even the necessary work you have chosen. Mindfulness will help you see that within the work and challenges of life are moments of wonder, beauty, and mystery. Your soul will respond with awe and gratitude. Wonder and gratitude are the threshold to love.

For some practical wisdom and exercises in mindfulness, see *Present Moment Wonderful Moment: Mindfulness Verses for Daily Living* by Thich Nhat Hahn. Another delightful book about living in the moment written for children of all ages is Jon J. Muth's *The Three Questions*.

A daily examen

The *examen* is a daily practice in which we reflect on God's presence in our lives and in the world. Adapted from the writings of Saint Ignatius of Loyola, it is a way of discerning God's presence in the ordinary.

In the evening find a quiet place to reflect on these aspects of your day:

- What were my desires during the day?
- Where did I experience them?

Using your imagination, choose a passage of scripture that matches the desire(s) you experienced.

Start a conversation with Jesus to reflect on what has moved you or caused you joy or sadness this day. Reflect on the feelings or thoughts that seemed to lead you to action today, including actions you regret, asking:

> ✍ In what ways could my actions have been done differently?
> ✍ In what ways should I respond to what moved me today, or not?

Become aware of a sense of consolation or comfort:

> ✍ Am I drawn to a desire or action as a result of what is nurturing me today?
> ✍ Am I ready to choose freely, to collaborate with God?

Express appreciation:

> ✍ Am I willing to stay with what I have chosen, to be transformed?

The *examen* is not a form of confession; it is a meditation on the day. Although I have laid it out as a step-by-step process, the exercises are actually interrelated and take place simultaneously most of the time. Nor is there time at the end of the day to make it a lengthy process. It should be an intentional yet flexible and even gentle process, taking about fifteen minutes.[10]

Journal writing
Writing in a personal journal can become an actual conversation with God. It is an opportunity to articulate what is happening within you and to reflect on significant aspects of each day. It will help you discern the spiritual dimension of daily events. Many persons keep a daily journal and others write only when they have time or inclination. One advantage of journal writing is that you may use an informal style and let the words speak uniquely for you. Regardless of frequency or style, jour-

naling is a form of personal prayer. It may be combined with the Ignatian *examen* mentioned above.

Henri Nouwen, who was a gifted spiritual writer, describes personal writing as a way "to give artistic expression to what we are living." He offers wise advice about this form of prayer: "Quite often a difficult, painful, or frustrating day can be 'redeemed' by writing about it. By writing we can claim what we have lived and thus integrate it more fully into our journeys."[11]

Creating prayers
God was the constant companion of the ancient Celtic Christians of Ireland, Wales, and Scotland. They acknowledged God's palpable presence everywhere. Their world was a single world—the realm of God. They lived close to the earth and were vulnerable to the blessings and dangers of the natural world. For them prayer and life were a continuous and identical pilgrimage, and God was their constant companion in the ordinary routines of daily life. The boundary between what we call "secular" and "sacred" was very thin. This awareness of God's presence and their need for protection, strength for holy living, forgiveness, and energy for survival were manifested in a series of short meditations embedded in the mundane personal activities, relationships, and needs that filled each day. Chants, prayers, invocations, songs, body movements, curses (expressing frustration and helplessness in the presence of persons with evil intent), and ceremonial actions were coupled to their daily needs. This is *unsophisticated* meditation, and that is its greatest strength. It needs no lofty theology, training, or approval. It is authentic because it is real.

In our busy and sophisticated twenty-first century, you may find you can benefit from expressing your desire for God and your awareness of God's presence in your mundane activities in similar, creative ways. Let your imagination become the womb of your praying. What would your prayers, chants, poetry, or invocations be like? One advantage to creating your own prayers is that you do not have to carry a book around with you! Your praying comes forth from what is already written on your heart. Do not rule out spontaneous prayers that emerge from daily tasks, situations, and desires, like these two examples of Celtic prayers.

> *As the home hearth fire was rekindled each morning:*
> I will kindle my fire this morning
> in the presence of the holy angels of heaven....
> God kindle thou in my heart within
> a flame of love to my neighbor,
> to my foe, to my friend, to my kindred all.

Try composing your own prayer as you turn up the thermostat, heat water for tea or coffee, or cook breakfast.

> *Walking to work, to hunt or fish, and returning home:*
> Bless to me, O God, the earth beneath my foot;
> Bless to me, O God, the path whereon I go;
> Bless to me, O God, the thing of my desire;
> Thou Evermore of evermore,
>   bless to me my rest.[12]

Try composing your own prayer as you go to and from your workplace.

In addition to creating your own prayers for the workplace, remember to be mindful as you begin each new task. It is so easy to just jump into the next phase of work. Throughout each day take a minute or two and remain in silence before you tackle the next task. Sit in front of the computer and offer what you are doing to God. Be mindful of the people you will see in the next staff meeting. Begin your next reading assignment or class with some deep breathing and quiet, even for less than a minute. Pause before you take out the trash, change a diaper, fold the laundry, or chop vegetables. Look at your child, spouse, or partner before you respond to what they are saying or doing. Take a breath in the midst of conflict. All these and more are meditation on life itself. As always, there is more to life than meets the eye. A great resource for meditation on simple daily tasks is Gunilla Norris's *Being Home.*

Lectio divina

Lectio divina means "divine or sacred reading," an ancient form of meditation found in many religious traditions. In the Christian tradition, its roots lie in the practices of the desert mothers and fathers that have evolved into an essential part of modern monastic prayer. It is now common for Christians in all walks of life. *Lectio divina* is a method for using the Bible as a path to discern God's presence and wisdom through listening and responding to God's voice in scripture. It is a discipline that invites us to look within and beyond the words to the One whose presence fills the earth.

The practice is easily learned, but takes repeated use to bear fruit.

(1) Find a relatively quiet place and sit with your back straight, but not rigid. Prior to beginning, choose a brief passage from the Bible—either one that is already familiar or one you have never seen before. During *lectio* you will read it slowly a total of four times, with a period of silence after each reading.

(2) After the first reading, listen in silence for a word or phrase that may attract your attention in a specific way. Remember and focus on that word or phrase.

(3) Read the passage a second time, and in the silence after the second reading, try to discern what

is happening in the passage and how you feel about what is happening or being said. What are your thoughts and sensations?

(4) After the third reading, listen in silence for awareness of what lies within or behind the passage and for any invitation, challenge, or wisdom it may offer you.

(5) After the fourth reading, simply sit in silence for five or ten minutes, without further reflection. Simply rest in God's presence and wisdom. When your silent period has ended, bring *lectio divina* to a close with an expression of thanks to God.

More advice about practicing *lectio divina* is found in Thelma Hall's *Too Deep for Words*, Norvene Vest's *No Moment Too Small*, and Michael J. Hansen, SJ's *The Gospels for Prayer*.

I have chosen to describe *lectio divina* last because it is one of the best examples of personal meditation and at the same time it combines features of meditation and contemplative prayer. It provides an excellent transition from meditation to contemplation. Perhaps you noticed that *lectio divina* uses silence in two ways. In the first two readings, you are listening in silence, but using your mind to see what is happening in the passage and discerning ways it may relate to your life. During the silence after the third reading, you are attentive to God's activity, rather than your own. After the final reading, you are silent with no activity, expectations, or thoughts. You have let go of control of the process and are simply present to God. This is contemplative prayer.

Chapter Eight

Contemplation

Contemplation may be described as a form of prayer without specific intention or purpose. It is a grace-filled, silent awareness of the mystery of God and an emptying of the mind's activity that leads a person to experience intimacy with God. This intimacy is the source of a change of consciousness that leads to love of God and neighbor. As we have seen, contemplation places aside our conscious control of thoughts, images, intent, words, and activity. An anonymous fourteenth-century English mystic described this process as entering a "cloud of unknowing" wherein we appear "naked of intent" before God. Through this silent and selfless listening we let go of control of what we think God is like and learn to desire God as God is. We let go, also, of our need for God to be the source of nurture, protection, healing, and wisdom for ourselves and for others. In contemplation we do not lose our individuality, but seek "nakedness" in God's presence so that we may see ourselves as we truly are, through God's eyes. We desire the union of our will with what God desires for us and for the world. This is not a renunciation of ourselves or of the world. In our nakedness and emptiness we experience an intimacy that transcends words and images.

It is hard to let go and take the risk of experiencing what we call "nothing." A poem by Rumi, a thirteenth-century Persian poet, speaks to this aspect of contemplation. "Speak little," the poet advises,

> Learn the words of eternity.
> Go beyond your tangled thoughts
>   and find the splendor of Paradise.
> Go beyond your little world
>   and find the grandeur of God's world.[13]

Contemplation is more difficult to explain than to experience because the *crux* of contemplative prayer is experience *beyond* words. It is an intimacy with God existing in a part of our human being that is beyond the confines of speech, thought, emotions, the senses, and conscious awareness. Many people are suspicious of contemplative prayer because it seems as though nothing is "happening" and there are no "results." We have difficulty trusting an intimacy with God and a movement of God's Spirit within us that is beyond conscious awareness and control.

It is not unusual for someone to try contemplative prayer and then return to meditation or no prayer at all. Contemplation deserves a reasonably long period of practice and a commitment to trusting the integrity of this discipline of prayer before its fruits will mature. Eventually it may lead to a profound change of consciousness and unsolicited fruits of the Spirit; it is challenging precisely because it requires a willingness to experience change.

The most profound change is that a sense of personal unity with all creation and living beings will replace the dualism of "me-and-the-rest-of-the-world." We will see and experience life in a different way. In the words of Saint Paul, "Do not be conformed to this world, but be transformed by the renewing of your minds, so that you may discern what is the will of God—what is good and acceptable and perfect" (Romans 12:2). At the same time it is a unique experience for each person.

At first I found it difficult to let go of control. My desire for results was completely unrealistic—a direct experience of God, solutions to all my problems, and wisdom to guide my spiritual growth! Reluctant to enter into the mystery of God's presence, I also experienced a touch of fear. I was not sure I liked mystery, preferring God on my own terms. But slowly, over the years, I learned that the mystery of God's essence is not something God has intentionally hidden or withheld from me. This essence is the aspect of God that transcends the boundaries of my human experience. Rather than a dense thicket that keeps me away from God, it is a mystery that leads me beyond time and space to a place of awe, wonder, and love. The mystery I experience in contemplative prayer is a threshold where time and space meet eternity. Like Moses meeting the mystery of God in the burning bush, on holy ground, I must take off my shoes. The silence of my nakedness before God is a burning bush that is never consumed.

After more than twenty years of practicing silent contemplative prayer in a variety of forms, I have learned that this prayer has three dimensions that will influence every person's spiritual transformation in some way:

(1) *Needing to listen:* As your mind slows down, you will learn to let go of all your inner chattering, needs, desires, and expectations. Then you will be able to hear God's voice more clearly in the uncluttered silence and emptiness.

(2) *Experiencing presence:* Your practice of contemplative prayer, as you persist in it day after day, will become the venue for your experience of God's presence. Gradually you will be transformed by the intimacy of this mutual presence.

(3) *Being transformed:* Contemplative prayer is not an end in itself. As you are slowly transformed by God in prayer, you will take what you have become, in God, into your daily life. The person you become with God in prayer is the same person you are called to be wherever you go. And the person you are in the midst of the people and tasks of your daily life is the same person who returns to prayer.

You will also learn that it is necessary for you to release control of your life as you enter contemplative prayer. As Jesus said, we must take up our cross and follow him. That means submitting your life to God, who loves you unconditionally. In my case, contemplation is a form of dying—it requires letting go of the habit of analytical thought that controls so much of my life. It means letting go of my need to control the outcome of my transformation and abandoning all efforts to "make something happen." Raimon Panikkar, a Roman Catholic priest, mystic, and philosopher, calls this form of letting go "the Discipline of the Three Silences":

- the silence of the intellect;
- the silence of the will;
- the silence of action.[14]

These three silences provide a temporary withdrawal from the conventional patterns of our daily lives, which in turn gives us a new perspective on life, a change of consciousness. Such withdrawal is not evasion of "real" life; it is a commitment to experiencing life in its fullness. It is a commitment to seeing as God sees. It is the womb of compassion.

The desert fathers and mothers called this state of non-attachment to any thing *apatheia* or "purity of heart"; for Abba Evagrius, it meant "to be without passion." In this context passion refers to unrestrained attachment and desire. Abba John Cassian used the phrase "purity of heart" to refer to a heart that is undivided in its longing for God and is unattached to anything except what God desires. A pure heart is a *spacious* heart that includes room for God and our neighbors. *Openness* of heart makes listening to God's Spirit possible, while a *flexible* heart can embody and share the fullness of God's love. This is a state of being that makes experience of God in contemplation possible without any desire to control the outcome. The heart becomes the center or axis where the physical, rational, and emotional dimensions of each person are united with and influenced by God's Spirit. The "horizontal" landscape of our finite daily living is permeated with the mysterious "vertical" realm of the Spirit. The breath of God vivifies every word and behavior. We become a whole person.

Contemplation is a form of prayer in which nothing is expected from us or by us. That makes it a difficult form of prayer in our twenty-first-century culture, which so values practical goals and results. A blessing at the end of the Eucharist begins, "The peace of God, which passes all understanding. . . . " And the reality behind this phrase is the heart of contemplative prayer, yet it runs counter to the intellect and the mind's rational categories. The discipline of contemplation is part of our pilgrimage toward becoming authentically human. It will help us transcend words, symbols, and creeds so that we will *experience* truth.

Contemplative prayer is a window to see and be seen by a dimension of divine reality that is usually hidden by our human limitations. It is like a full eclipse of the sun. The sun's energy, literally our source of life, is so powerful we cannot look at its full intensity or experience its radiation all at once. The inability of our eyes to absorb such radiation without permanent damage means that we miss seeing its beauty with the naked eye. But every two years the combination of the earth's rotation and orbit and the moon's orbit places the moon directly in front of our view of the sun. During a full solar eclipse the moon's presence makes the sun's amazing corona visible, although even then we must use solar filters to protect our eyes. Like flames in a fireplace, colorful streaks of coronal gas shoot from the sun's surface. Electrified hydrogen dashes into space at the speed of light. This ballet of light and movement is usually hidden from us by the sun's immense radiation. For seven minutes, every two years, it is possible to experience a sacred dance that remains, literally, a blinding mystery.

SUGGESTIONS FOR SILENT CONTEMPLATIVE PRAYER

Contemplative prayer may be practiced in a variety of forms and there are only two requirements: desire and persistence. Its purpose is awareness and not achievement; it opens us to the possibility of finding God's presence in all things. This vision of the sacred dimension of life will guide the stewardship of our own lives, our relationships, our work, and our use of creation. It will challenge us to live responsible and compassionate lives.

Contemplative prayer and meditation show us the incarnation of God in the present moment. They fulfill Jesus' promise to "come again" and shift our vision away from our endless expectations and plans toward the eternal presence of God in time and space. When we are willing to let go of control of our thoughts and actions, we will not have to search for God. God is already present and waiting for us.

In contemplative prayer everyone is a beginner and the methods are simple. There are a number of good books about contemplative prayer and they may be helpful, but there is no substitute for contemplative prayer itself. If you have no experience of contemplative prayer it may be helpful to find a group within your own tradition and begin with them. A few useful books are listed in the resources guide at the end of this book. I will describe here three examples of the many forms of contemplative prayer.

Simple sitting
Find a relatively quiet place in your home, your workplace, a church, mosque, or synagogue, a park or another favorite place. You will need a chair, bench, or floor space to sit comfortably with your back straight and supported, but not rigid. With your eyes closed or partially open, begin breathing slowly in and out. Be conscious of your pattern of deep breathing. Let your body and your mind become as relaxed as possible. As your mind becomes relaxed you will experience many thoughts passing rapidly through your mind. These thoughts are normal. Let them come and go. Try, as best you can, to let your mind and inner being become empty. Let your whole being be an open vessel for God's presence and voice. Avoid expectations or hoped-for outcomes. Simply be present to God.

Some people find it helpful to repeat a word or short phrase silently to help let go of distracting thoughts and bring themselves back to quietness of mind. You can choose a word that has special meaning to you. You might want to repeat a name for God, such as "Holy One," or a short request, such as "Come, Holy Spirit," but try not to think about the intellectual meaning of the words. When you have sat in silence for about twenty minutes, open your eyes, wait for a minute or two, and then give thanks to God at the end of your meditation.

Centering prayer
This method is similar to "simple sitting," but may begin with reading Holy Scripture. Set aside twenty minutes.

Find a relatively quiet place and sit with your back straight, but not rigid. Let your body and mind become as relaxed as possible. Close your eyes and begin to settle down in God who dwells at the center of your being. You may read a short passage from the Bible and then allow yourself to become silent in mind, body, and spirit. Begin a pattern of deep breathing. Use a one- or two-syllable word to symbolize your desire to go to God, and repeat that word whenever you sense your mind is drifting. Thoughts are normal. Let them come, accept them, and let them go. After twenty minutes conclude your silence by reciting a short prayer from your own tradition or from the Bible. (This form of centering prayer follows the pattern taught by Thomas Keating in *Open Mind, Open Heart.*)

Contemplative walking
Find a place where you can have relative quiet and space for walking, such as a park or an empty church. Stand motionless, begin a deep rhythm of breathing and let yourself become relaxed in body, mind, and spirit. When you feel that you are centered, slowly begin walking, taking small steps and keeping your feet roughly parallel with your shoulders. Walk slowly, with a rhythm that allows your feet to alternate touching the ground without stopping between steps. (Remember, there is no right or wrong way.) Continue your deep breathing as you walk.

Remember that each step is the only step, and that each moment is the only moment to be in the presence of God. Be aware of each foot's gentle contact with the earth, carpet, or floor. Relax your mind and become aware of objects that appear as you walk, but do not try to evaluate or analyze them. Let them be what they are as you encounter them.

Relax your jaw muscles by assuming a half-smile and continue walking without intention, destination, or purpose. When distractions or thoughts appear, try counting the number of steps you take as you inhale and exhale. This may help restore you to a relaxed attentiveness.

When you wish to end the walking, stop and continue your deep breathing for a minute or two. Offer thanks to God and resume your other activities. Contemplative walking can be very short, but it is best to allow fifteen to twenty minutes. Once in a while, try this form of contemplative prayer for an hour. (This description of contemplative walking is influenced by the teaching of Thich Nhat Hanh in *The Long Road Turns to Joy: A Guide to Walking Meditation.*)

CREATING AN ENVIRONMENT AND DISCIPLINE FOR PRAYER

When the author of *The Cloud of Unknowing* said, "Prayer is naught else but a naked intent directed unto God," he or she knew it is hard to remain in such "naked" prayer. There are a variety of actions, disciplines, and atmospheres that can provide a transition into and assist us in silent, wordless, imageless contemplation. These may be seen as, in the phrase of Thomas Hand, "clothes for the movement of the heart."[15]

There are two types of contemplation that are helpful for most people: centering prayer and simple sitting (called *zazen* in the Zen Buddhist tradition). In both types of prayer the following aids can facilitate the movement of the heart:

    🖋 place;

    🖋 posture;

    🖋 breathing;

    🖋 the use of a word or phrase;

    🖋 simple musical rhythms, such as the sound of a meditation bell, drumming, and chanting.

These aids to contemplation are helpful because the movement from verbal to contemplative prayer is difficult and full of distractions. It is a movement from prayer of the mind to prayer of the heart, and can, at times, be painful because it demands that we be open and vulnerable. These aids can help us direct attention away from ourselves and remove the intentions, fears, façades, and personal expectations with which we mask our inner being.

Place

Jesus told his followers, "Whenever you pray, go into your room and shut the door and pray to your Father who is in secret; and your Father who sees in secret will reward you" (Matthew 6:6). Origen, a third-century Christian scholar and mystic in Alexandria, reminds us, "Any place can be suitable for prayer: it becomes so as soon as one prays well it in. . . . If we want to pray quietly without being disturbed, we may choose a particular place in our own house, if there is space—a consecrated place, so to speak—and pray there." For extended periods of contemplation choose a place where there will be little or no chance for interruptions. Rarely can we find a place where we can eliminate all noise and distractions, but we need to be free from anything that will break up our period of silence. You might be able to set aside a room or part of a room in your house for this purpose, but you also may have to use whatever space is available and temporarily free of other people.

Within the space we choose for regular contemplation there can be four areas of focus: *fire, earth, water,* and *air.* These elements will help create a small area, along with a cross, icon, or work of art, that draws us further into our desire for God, a gateway to experience Truth.

The presence of one or two candles will add an atmosphere of warmth and reverence. The lighting and then extinguishing of candles can initiate and bring closure to the time of silence. Fire has always been a symbol of God's presence and reminds Christians that Christ brings light to the world and enlightens our consciousness. Some people prefer a darkened space for contemplation, but the presence of natural light, except at night, can remind us that the same boundary that creates our space for silence is also the boundary that connects us to the rest of the world. Incense is less commonly used, but its smoke is a visible symbol that prayer is not static, and its fragrance helps set this space apart for the purpose of prayer.

Other helpful additions to an atmosphere for prayerful silence are a green plant and a bowl of water. The plant is a sign of God's creative verdancy and the soil that surrounds it reminds us of the earth, the source of our life and continued physical sustenance. A bowl of water, placed at the entrance of the room or the area set aside for meditation, is a sign that we are passing through a boundary that leads to an inner journey of transformation—as is the water of baptism for Christians. Touching the water and making the sign of the cross on our forehead can be a physical act that begins a process of centering as we make a transition from our active lives to a time of contemplative prayer.

The final element in an atmosphere of contemplation is already in every space we use: air. The air is invisible and a sign of the limitlessness of God as well as a sign of God's life and Spirit within us. Each breath in silent prayer is a sign of God's presence.

The soil that surrounds the plant, the air, the candlelight, and the bowl of water: earth, air, fire, and water—the basic elements of life—are present as we enter a journey to experience the Source of life.

Posture

Some people prefer to sit in a simple chair with a padded seat (but not an "easy chair"), while others sit directly on the floor with their legs underneath on a meditation cushion (*zabuton*) and a meditation pillow (*zafu*). Another possibility is a "halfway" position that uses a small bench-like device (called a "prayer bench") that allows you to sit with your back supported while your knees and legs rest on the floor, extending behind you under the bench. Or you may want to use an assortment of cushions to help you achieve the desired posture.

Regardless of which method you use, the posture assumed should enable you to be comfortable, relaxed, and attentive. *Comfortable* means a posture that does not produce distracting pain or fatigue, regardless of reason. Whether on the floor or in a chair, you should have a degree of comfort that will allow you to become unaware of your body. This does not mean rejecting the body, but simply recognizing the body's cooperation in prayer. We do not cease being embodied creatures even though we seek experience of God, which transcends yet permeates the physical. However, the comfort level should enhance contemplation but not put you to sleep. It is important to assume a posture in which your back is straight, but not rigid or tense. This takes weight off your diaphragm and will help the flow of breathing.

By *relaxed* I mean a comfortable posture that permits you to rest your mind and your body. Beginning with facial muscles, it is possible to let go of muscle tension and continue to let your muscles help support your posture, but without tensing them. Let the muscles of your jaw and shoulders relax. Your shoulders should be low and not "up tight." In Zen Buddhist silent contemplation, people are invited to "put a half-smile on their faces." If you smile just enough to part your lips, you will notice your jaw muscles and entire face relax. This is important since a tensing of the jaw usually accompanies worry, intense thought, or anger. A relaxed posture can assist you in letting go of mental as well as physical tension and focus.

Attentive means a demeanor of openness and waiting. Your focus is away from yourself to what is at work in your heart. Being attentive means a willingness to "come and see" rather than control the experience of God in contemplation. Attentiveness does not mean renouncing your individuality, but a willingness to be vulnerable, to be acted upon. It is the desire to direct your whole being toward the experience of God in a naked and mutual seeing. Your body, through a comfortable, relaxed, and attentive posture, is an integral part of contemplation.

Breathing

Your breathing is a constant sacrament of God's presence. In Hebrew the word for breath, wind, and spirit have the same root: *ruach.* Most of the time you are not conscious of your breathing, yet it is your constant companion and without it you would die. Breathing is a symbol of God's presence, a physical process which helps you relax and become centered, and can be an effective transition from your normal active behavior into contemplative experience of God.

Once you have become relaxed in a comfortable posture, breathing can help you become attentive and lead you into a deeper experience of relaxation from the anxiety and chatter that begins to invade your mind in contemplation. Many people find it helpful to use the "half-smile"; inhale through your nose very slowly until the lungs are full, then, without stopping, exhale completely through your mouth. In the first few minutes, or longer, of each period of contemplation repeat this breathing cycle slowly and deliberately, remaining conscious of the movement of your breath through the complete cycle.

In a way which cannot be explained, this consciousness of your breath can bring an awareness of the presence of God's Spirit and life in you. It will also help you become more relaxed, become freer from distractions, and more attentive.

Eventually you will no longer be aware of your breathing and will lose awareness of your body as well. This enhanced degree of attentiveness will enable you to be present before God without distractions. When distractions return, as they do for everyone, begin your conscious cycle of breathing again. Do not worry about the need to cough or other involuntary physical needs, discomforts, or noises. Just let them happen and "pass by," and go on with your deep cycle and rhythm of breathing.

The use of a word or phrase
Most people find the repetition of a word or phrase as useful as the cycle of breathing. The integration of the rhythm of breathing and the word or phrase can be a powerful aid to contemplative silence, especially as a transition from our verbal, emotional, and mental experience of God to a wordless and imageless form of contemplation. Some continue the use of the word or phrase throughout contemplation—although losing conscious attention to the words themselves—while others use the words to lead them beyond the words, which eventually cease to be repeated.

Many people who are new to silent contemplation are reluctant to use these mantras, either because they seem contrived or because of their strong association with the spiritual traditions of the East, especially Hinduism and Zen Buddhism. But there is nothing "magical" about mantras and their purpose is not to conjure up religious experience of any kind. Mantras are part of the technique for becoming attentive to God, not manipulating God. They have been part of many religious traditions, including the Christian tradition, for thousands of years. Even the desert fathers and mothers refer to the use of a mantra—a "monologist" or one-word or one-phrase prayer.

The purpose of repetition is related to the rhythm of our prayer and not to an effort to bombard God with our desires or needs. The mantra, with or without a melody that is chanted, creates a rhythmic pattern of attentiveness and can be an effective transition from activity of body and mind into an experience of God that does not depend on us, our expectations and concerns. Rhythm is an integral part of all art that transcends words and images—that exists not for its own sake, but for what it evokes within us. The rhythm achieved through repetition of the mantra can be a gateway into the contemplative experience of God that helps to integrate the physical and the spiritual.

Some people use one word for a mantra, such as the many names for God in scripture, or simply repeat "Jesus" or the Aramaic phrase *Ma-ranatha*, which means "Come, Lord." Others use some variation of the Jesus Prayer ("Lord Jesus Christ, have mercy on me") or "Holy, Holy, Holy One," "Come, Holy, Holy," "Come, Holy Spirit," or other phrases that resonate with their spirit. Try to avoid thinking about the word or phrase, its literal meaning or significance. Many people find the mantra an essential part of contemplative prayer, and the only way to discover what a mantra is and whether it will assist your contemplation is to use it.

Simple muscial rhythms
The use of a small drum, either by itself or with a simple chant, is similar to the use of a mantra, but is not necessarily a substitute. Like breathing and use of a mantra, the act of drumming, with or without accompanying chant, can be a transition into contemplation. It marks

the beginning and end of many kinds of contemplative prayer. The effectiveness of rhythm in initiating attentiveness, relaxation, and focus has been discussed already. Music has been an integral part of every religious tradition. Drumming is appropriate for contemplative prayer because its rhythm reminds us of the rhythm of the beating of our hearts and the rhythms of life itself, such as the four seasons, night and day, the ebb and flow of the tides, and human birth and death.

The sound of a meditation bell creates a transition from activity into the silence of contemplative prayer. The sound of the bell becomes a melodic mantra that may help bring about heightened awareness: when the bell "speaks" we are led to an attentive demeanor leading toward awareness of God's presence. A bell may also be used to mark transitions during a period of contemplative prayer and bring the session to a close.

Chanting serves the same purpose as mantras and drumming. It is especially helpful as a transition from a cognitive and verbal focus on God, which is the result of meditating on a passage of scripture, to imageless contemplation. Chanting may be done by one person alone, but it is most powerful when a group is experiencing silent contemplation together. As in Gregorian chant, there are three "levels" within the action of chanting:

 the *conscious* level, which focuses us on the words;

 the *mantric* level, in which the rhythm of repetition takes us beyond the literal meaning of the words;

 the *contemplative* level, at which we experience the presence of God beyond all words and images.

Chanting and drumming may be combined, but it is important to distinguish between this type of chanting and the use of music for worship and praise. The rhythm of percussion in music of praise is a legitimate and effective form of meditation in other settings, but the use of drumming and chanting can become a transition from feelings and thoughts to a more contemplative experience of God. The rhythm of a simple drumbeat enhances attentiveness and its rhythm reminds us of our heartbeats and the flow of God's life within us. Both experiences of percussion are valid, but each serves a different form of prayer. It is not a "better" way, but a different way.

SUMMING UP

These "clothes for the movement of the heart" have proven to be helpful to many people. They are ancient garments that have been tried on and worn by countless numbers of people, and they have stood the test of constant and authentic use. Whether or not they will assist your contemplation will depend on you—some of them may, and some may not.

If you are unfamiliar with any kind of contemplative practice, you may have difficulty developing a personal pattern of contemplation simply from a book or manual like this one. What will help you most is the experience of contemplation in a group and the advice, assistance, and reflection of others who are trying to follow the same path. At the same time, it is important to remember that learning the discipline of contemplation in a group is a powerful experience, and you will need to resist the impulse to depend too much on the group experience. The practice of both individual and group contemplation are equally valid experiences, so silent prayer in groups should complement your regular pattern of private contemplative prayer and not become a substitute for it.

Chapter 9

Persistence

In *The Feminine Face of God,* the authors write about a woman who once told her father, "My baptism didn't take!" Later she asked him, "Suppose somebody could believe some of the doctrine, but not all of it. Would that mean they weren't a Christian?" He responded immediately, "You don't have to understand the mystery of God to be a Christian. But you have to practice. If you wait until all the understanding comes before practicing, you'll never understand. It's the practice that gives rise to understanding. So practice, practice, practice!"[16]

Rest in God . . . day after day
In the fourth century the desert fathers and mothers of Egypt described their meditation as *quies,* "resting in God." They knew that rest, quiet, and stillness are not static or passive. They learned that in meditation we find ourselves *in God,* by going beyond the boundaries we set for ourselves to discover a new way of living in this world.

Jesus said, "If your eye is healthy [single], your whole body will be full of light" (Matthew 6:22). This new way of living is called "enlightenment." In the Christian tradition, enlightenment is not "leaving" this world nor seeking a "better" world, but becoming aware of and living into the fullness of *this life* here on earth. The term *quies* shows us the completeness of our present life by enabling us to see life through the template of God's vision.

Simone Weil calls meditation the way of "selfless attention." We do not seek what is good, nor do we seek our own transformation. We rest our consciousness in the consciousness of God. We desire what God desires. We depend entirely on God.

One day at a time . . . day after day

Contemplative prayer and meditation are about the incarnation of God in the present moment. They fulfill Jesus' promise to "come again." They shift our vision away from endless expectations, planning, and evaluation of life to experience the eternal presence of God within time and space. If you are willing to let go of control of your thoughts and actions, you will not have to search for God. Each moment is a new opportunity to discern and remain in God's presence. You are always a beginner!

Let go of control . . . over and over again

Jesus said, "For those who want to save their life will lose it, and those who lose their life for my sake will find it" (Matthew 16:25). Until we are willing to be rooted and grounded in God, our lives will always be limited and incomplete. Our society does not value the idea of "letting go" or the word "surrender"; everything around us compels us to cling to what is futile, shallow, and unreal. We are afraid to be touched by God because we fear that something might happen that lies beyond what we can secure and protect. We have forgotten that fullness of life requires a letting go of all that hinders us from living in the presence of God. In contemplative prayer and meditation we seek emptiness so that in our daily lives we will be able to discern what is truly empty of life and unreal. And as we let go of our need to control the outcome of contemplative prayer, our hearts will expand and in that spaciousness we will receive the energies of God's Spirit.

Salvation is "being on the way" to the realm of God that already exists within us. This divine presence is the source of our most authentic self. To find ourselves we must look within and learn to know ourselves as God knows us. Jesus said, "It is the pleasure of the Holy One to give you the realm of God" (Luke 12:32, my translation). It is a gift to be reopened every day of our lives.

Stay centered... day after day
As I said earlier, the Latin word from which we get "meditation" has to do with "remaining in the center." The Christian tradition teaches that the Spirit of God already dwells in our center, as when Jesus spoke of going into our "inner room" (NASB) to pray, and seeking the pearl of great price. He told his followers, "Abide in me as I abide in you" (John 15:4). The Latin root for the word "contemplation" is *con-templum. Templum* refers to an "open space" or "temple," so contemplation is the desire to remain "in the temple," in your own heart and in the heart of God. If we lose sight of God we will lose sight of what it means to be human. Saint Catherine of Genoa said, "I know myself in God," and Saint Augustine echoed her thought: "If I am not in God, then I am not at all." Remain in the company of God each new day.

Relax about "progress"... day after day
A ninth-century Welsh poem about creation contains an important truth for us:

> The Father created the world by a miracle;
> It is difficult to express its measure.
> Letters cannot contain it,
> letters cannot comprehend it.[17]

This poem reminds us that Christianity is not primarily a message, but the experience of life in union with God, as we are led by the risen Christ. God's life-giving Word is spoken through human lives regardless of our religious tradition. Yet as we travel the spiritual path we are constantly tempted to impose our culture's values of success and failure on our life of prayer. We are pressured to look for "progress": *Is this working? What am I getting from this? Am I still sinful? Am I becoming holier? What can I do about my lack of progress? Where is the latest book or program to help me?*

Contemplative prayer and meditation are opportunities to go beyond this self-centered obsession with productivity and depend solely on God instead. They enable us to listen to God's voice with an open heart. As we hear that voice, day after day, in the stillness and openness of contemplation and meditation, we will learn to recognize and trust that same voice in the midst of our daily lives and recognize God's presence in the surrounding world.

To Sum It Up

🖉 Contemplative prayer and meditation should be simple.

🖉 Your attitude is essential: openness, a sense of wonder, a faithful commitment, and the persistence of discipline.

🖉 Let go of anxiety about what will happen in silence. Contemplation places us in the heart of God, where all fear is cast out.

🖉 You will never become an expert! Contemplation and meditation are ordinary and simple disciplines, open to everyone, not just for "specialists."

🖉   Let go of expectations. When you are distracted and bored, do not try to "fix" the situation, but be as relaxed as you can.

🖉   You don't have to be "acceptable" or "worthy" to meditate. All that you are is open to God in contemplative prayer, your failures as well as your faithfulness, your fears as well as your joys, your anger as well as your hopefulness.

🖉   Meditation and contemplation are not related in any way to magic or conjuring a personally desired end. Do not try to be in control. Be present. That is all!

🖉   Do not rely on what other persons say, write, or teach. As helpful as this may be, you must experience God yourself, and commit yourself to the disciplines of meditation and contemplative prayer.

🖉   The only things you need for contemplative prayer and meditation are desire and persistence; there is no substitute for practice, practice, and more practice—not out of duty but out of love.

Chapter 10

Transformation

Prayer will change the way you live. The time you spend with God in prayer will form you as a person. This process is sometimes called *sanctification*. That does not mean that you become a "holier-than-thou" kind of person, but that gradually, over time, your life will voluntarily conform to God's desires for you. You are already created in God's image, and your vocation as a Christian is to manifest the likeness of God in the way you live.

Prayer is an opportunity to place yourself in God's presence. It is the landscape of your personal relationship with God. It has many forms and may take place at any time or location. As you place yourself in God's presence you will eventually discover that you are becoming rooted and grounded in divine love. The Christian way to discover what this love is like is to look at the life of Jesus in the four gospels. As Saint Paul said, Jesus is the manifestation of God's love in human form (Colossians 1:15–20). Your time in prayer will gradually help you see yourself through God's eyes (your true self) and the love you experience in prayer will become tangible in every aspect of your daily life. This will influence study, teaching, writing, work, family, relationships, care of the earth and your possessions, and your awareness of the need for justice and responsible living.

Saint Paul called this "life in Christ" (see 1 Corinthians 12:1–11 and Galatians 2:20). You can live *in God*, within the limitations and conditions of human life. When Jesus said, "Be perfect, therefore, as your heavenly Father is perfect" (Matthew 5:48), he did not mean that you should be morally pure in some ideal sense. The accurate meaning of "perfect" as Jesus used it is to "move toward completion." In this context "perfect" means to become fully and truly yourself.

Your perfection is also "a work in process." Through prayer, God's grace collaborates with your desires and spiritual gifts as you move toward the fullness of who you are—within the challenges, limitations, and possibilities of daily life. It is a mysterious process that will never end. Mystery is an aspect of life that draws us beyond what we can define or control. It is a gift of God. Prayer will help you keep on this path and resist influences and temptations that will misdirect your steps and scatter your soul. God invites you, every day, to collaborate in the creation of your life as if it were a work of art. It will take time and discipline and cannot be rushed. When you take wrong steps, God waits to invite you back on the path. Remember, there is nothing you can do to rush a sunrise!

CHALLENGES AND DIFFICULTIES OF PRAYING

So far we have reflected on the advantages of personal prayer, but we should not ignore its difficulties, challenges, and responsibilities. Although praying is relatively simple, it is not easy. Praying does not occur in a vacuum. We live in complex environments that include many influences that are beyond our control. It is important to recognize that praying does not make us "perfect" even though we earnestly desire progress in our life with God. Praying takes place in the midst of our yet-to-be-completed humanity and the natural limitations of human, finite existence.

Theologian G. K. Chesterton insisted that Christianity has not been "tried and found wanting"—it has been found difficult and *not* tried. When we make our religious life comfortable we are leaving out its demands and challenges. The desert mother Syncletica reminds us that the transformation of prayer does not take place all at once, and she encourages us to persist when it becomes difficult. "In the beginning there are a great many battles and a good bit of suffering for those who are advancing towards God and afterwards, ineffable joy. It is like those who wish to light a fire; at first they are choked by the smoke and cry, and by this means obtain what they seek (as it is said: 'Our God is a consuming fire' [Hebrews 12:24]). So we must also kindle the divine fire in ourselves through tears and work." The "divine fire in ourselves" becomes the pathway toward "ineffable joy."

Here are three aspects of prayer that many people have found difficult and challenging:

(1) Trusting that something is happening and that it is worth the effort.

(2) Taking the risk of being transformed and letting go of control of the outcome.

(3) Accepting the responsibilities and challenges of our transformed life and intimacy with God.

Trusting that something is happening
Trust or faith in God is placing your life in God's hands. Trust, like hope, is not a simplistic belief that everything will turn out according to plan. It is the awareness that your relationship with God in prayer is real and worth the effort *regardless of the outcome.* There will be many times when you are not aware of God's presence and are sure that nothing is happening as a result of your prayer.

This is partly because prayer is a relationship that leads you beyond your mind and your emotions. It is hard to accept the reality of something you cannot define or control. "Where are you, God?" is a legitimate prayer.

I remember something that happened during the first year of my seminary training to become an Episcopal priest. I was part of a Gregorian chant choir singing in sanctuary of the Cathedral of Saint John the Divine in New York City. The setting was beautiful and inspiring until the moment I asked myself, "What if all this is a hoax?" At that moment I failed to trust what I could *not* see in the midst of the beauty I could see. Was something *really* happening? Over the past forty-six years of contemplative prayer and meditation I have had "watershed" experiences where God's presence was palpable and the experience brought obvious changes in my living. But most of my praying has resulted in "empty buckets." This does not mean my prayer was empty or that there were no consequences. I was not *conscious* of anything happening. By maintaining my discipline of praying, I came to trust that at a deep and mysterious level of my being something *really was happening.* Trusting the mystery of prayer is not easy. Like any important relationship, it is more about faithfulness than "progress."

Taking the risk of prayer
When you pray you are submitting yourself to the influence and power of One who loves you without conditions. There is nothing you can do to make God love you more than God loves you at this moment. There is nothing you can do to make God love you less than God loves you at this moment. This is worth repeating!

Prayer is one way of saying, "I can't make it on my own." This is why Jesus said you must die to yourself in order to find yourself. Every person works really hard to make himself or herself into the person he or she wants to be. But only God knows who you truly are. As you "crucify" or die to being in charge of your life, you will discover who you really are. This is what the death of Jesus can teach us. Jesus did not have to die to show us the nature of God's love. His life did that beautifully. Yet his commitment to the lives of people around him who were being marginalized and abused led to his "speaking truth to power." It was his hope, too, that honest words to those who were the cause of injustice would transform their lives and help heal society. Jesus took the risk of love, knowing it might lead to his own marginalization and death. He had to accept the risks of manifesting God's love and desire for justice. It was love that led to his crucifixion. It was Jesus' authenticity of life that led to his death, and in that death we can see the extent of God's love for all people. When Jesus invites us to "die" to ourselves he is exhorting us to have this kind of loving authenticity. He knows why we were created.

Jesus' death does not change God's mind about you. God already loves you unconditionally. Jesus' death can change your mind about *yourself*. The cross of Jesus will draw you into an awesome demonstration of God's love for you and set you on a path to make that same love tangible in your life. When you wear a cross you are not only displaying a symbol of God's love for the world, you are declaring that you have accepted God's invitation to love every person who sees the cross you are wearing. That is the risk of love and the risk of prayer.

Accepting the responsibilities and challenges of prayer
It is important to remember that you have *chosen* to embrace the responsibilities and challenges that flow from your life of prayer. They are not things you are *required* to do. They spring freely from your love of God and your neighbor. You *want* to fulfill them. But that does not mean they are easy or that you will always be in the

mood. Sometimes it is hard to discern what you are being called to say or do. That is another reason to remain in the company of God.

Prayer will help you see yourself, God, and the world more honestly. It will help you be real by showing your natural goodness, and at the same time help you discern ways God is calling you to change and mature. Prayer will change your consciousness so that you will see into the deeper meaning of what is going on in your life and the world around you. It will bring you joy at the wonder of creation and the amazing creativity and variety of human beings. Prayer will also bring you sadness and righteous anger at the presence of injustice, hunger, and unnecessary conflict and abuse of other human beings. Your time apart with God will reveal ways you can speak out in response and become involved in the needs of others. Prayer will also let you know when you have become a source of pain or injustice for other persons. Prayer is not self-centered "navel-gazing" that separates you from life. It will drive you to become more fully engaged with life in the same way that the Spirit of God drove Jesus into the wilderness to pray and then out into the lives of people around him. This is the challenge of love.

As you remain faithful in your life with God you will receive both the desire and strength to love your neighbor and rejoice in the goodness of life. You will know what is real and not be satisfied with what is not real. When Jesus said, "Take up your cross and follow me," he was really saying, "Let your life be your message!"

Remaining faithful means staying with your pattern of daily prayer. Remain in the company of God in the midst of your unbelievably busy days. As you learn to listen to God's voice regularly, you will learn to recognize God's voice everywhere and trust what you are hearing. Jesus said, "Abide in me as I abide in you.... Those who abide in me and I in them bear much fruit, because apart from me you can do nothing" (John 15:4–5).

Prayer is more than words. It is the demeanor of a humble and flexible heart that makes space in your life for God and other people. This is why we sometimes kneel to pray. We know that we are not the center of the universe. In one of her letters, Etty Hillesum, a Jewish writer who perished in the Holocaust, expresses her sudden, mysterious impulse to kneel: "A desire to kneel down sometimes pulses through my body, or rather it is as if my body has been meant and made for the act of kneeling. Sometimes, in moments of deep gratitude, kneeling down becomes an overwhelming urge, head deeply bowed, hands before my face."[18]

But whether you kneel or not, if you are bowing in spirit you will begin to see the inner reality and sanctity of people and things. We can pray for each other, along with the author of the letter to the Ephesians: "I pray that you may have the power to comprehend, with all the saints, what is the breadth and length and height and depth, and to know the love of Christ that surpasses knowledge, so that you may be filled with all the fullness of God" (3:18–19).

The consequence of prayer is that in submitting yourself voluntarily to God, you are changed. It is no longer you who live, but Christ who lives in you (Galatians 2:20). You become real. You become the beloved person you were created to be. Love is the meaning.

WHAT HAPPENS WHEN I FAIL TO LOVE?

Prayer includes being honest about yourself. Both your goodness and your sins tell you what direction your life is taking. They show you how you are responding or failing to respond to God's invitation to manifest God's love in your life. A sin is anything that inhibits or denies your love of God, your neighbor, yourself, and creation. Some sins have more serious consequences than others, but all sins place roadblocks on your path to being who you truly are in Christ. They also create self-made barriers between you, other people, and God, even though God's love and closeness to you remain unchanged. When this happens it is important to be honest about what you have done. This will help you, in your prayer, to express disappointment and sorrow about your behavior.

As it is written in the first letter of John, "If we say that we have no sin, we deceive ourselves, and the truth is not in us. If we confess our sins, he who is faithful and just will forgive us our sins and cleanse us from all unrighteousness" (1 John 1:8–9). Sin does not change God's love for us, but it grieves God to see us reject the path of love, even temporarily. The writer is not trying to condemn us because we can be sinful persons. Instead he reminds us that *how we live* makes a huge difference to God, to ourselves, to other people, and to creation. This is why prayer will make a difference in our lives.

When you acknowledge your sins you are taking a first step back toward your vocation to manifest God's love in your life. This is called *repentance* and is necessary because it will "turn your life around" and open you, once again, to God's assistance and guidance to walk the path of love. God's forgiveness does not eliminate what you have done. It is God's willingness to accept you *as you are* and to collaborate with you once again, by offering God's grace and creative energy. Forgiveness restores the close relationship you desire with God. It is a return to your true self and unloads the negative feelings and guilt that make it so hard to see yourself as God sees you. You are freed to love as God loves.

DEPENDING ON GOD

We have been "freed to love."[19] To me this is one of the most profound statements of the core of the Christian gospel that exists. Sometimes this vocation leads to difficult places and situations, and you will not be sure what to do. Where can you go for help? Here is advice from the author of the first letter of Peter: "For to this you have been called, because Christ also suffered for you, leaving you an example, so that you should follow in his steps" (1 Peter 2:21). Peter tells you to follow in Jesus' steps. Prayer will help you hear the sound of those steps and turn to Jesus for help.

Can you tune your ears to the sound of Christ's footsteps in every aspect of your daily life? In the second chapter of Genesis we read that shortly after Adam and Eve decided to take full control of their lives and eat fruit from the tree of the knowledge of good and evil, they heard God walking in the garden of Eden. Their response was to hide themselves because they knew their disobedience had changed their intimate relationship with God. Now they feared God's presence. Jesus wants you to know that you do not have to hide from God under any circumstances, especially if you have strayed from the path of love or need help when life gets difficult.

If you want to follow Jesus, *listen to his footsteps.* If you have chosen to walk away from the path of love, the sound of his footsteps will help you find your way back. If you need encouragement to remain on the path because you are not sure where it is leading, Jesus' footsteps will remind you to seek his strength and wisdom. But his footsteps will be very difficult to hear if you do not take time to listen. This is why prayer is important. Jesus calls each of us to wait and pray, even for brief moments every day. Prayer is more about listening than talking. There are many ways to listen.

You Are God's Field

"For we are God's servants, working together; you are God's field, God's building" (1 Corinthians 3:9). Perhaps Saint Paul had Jesus' parable of the mustard seed in mind when he used the image of a field to describe our life with God. Jesus said, "The kingdom of heaven is like a mustard seed that someone took and sowed in his field; it is the smallest of all the seeds, but when it has grown it is the greatest of shrubs and becomes a tree, so that the birds of the air come and make nests in its branches" (Matthew 13:31–32). God has sown a tiny seed within you, and God is the mysterious power that will make it grow and mature. You may wonder whether or not you can make a difference in the world. "What is the seed growing within me, compared to the needs of God's kingdom?" is a normal question. Yet what may seem small in human terms has the potential to become "the greatest of shrubs." Your life can produce a tree in which other people will come and "make nests in its branches." Nests are the environments for new life. Your life may seem small, but you are the fertile ground for the realm of God's life in the world.

Transformation

Transformation is the ever-evolving development of your true self through a life of prayer. The phrase "life of prayer" infers that prayer will not be a sector of your life that is separate from family, work, recreation, faith community, education, and social issues, but is rather your intentional openness to God. Prayer, as we have seen, may include imageless contemplative prayer, meditation and reflection, *lectio divina*, centering prayer, wonder, and gratitude for life. It can be embodied through specific spiritual disciplines such as discernment, intercession, praise, body prayer, corporate liturgical worship, self-awareness, spiritual friendship, spiritual direction, openness to self-knowledge, study, creative expression, and a firm desire for constant growth that leads away from self-reliance and self-centeredness. Your life of prayer will lead you deeper into the heart of God and at the same time deeper into the life of the world.

In your prayer you will experience God's unconditional love, and that experience will become the womb of your compassionate love of others. Your life of prayer will enable you to grow in unique knowledge that is the fruit of silence and presence to God. This knowledge is different from cognitive knowledge and will integrate all other knowledge and experience. Contemplative knowledge is born in your heart and will inform and empower your whole being with the power of love. Your life of prayer will make it possible to listen with the ears of your heart and discern with the mind of Christ. You will know what is real.

This always-new transformation of consciousness is your sacred "work," and with God's grace, it will sanctify all your desires, thoughts, words, and work. It is a treasure that will make it possible for you to collaborate with God in the creation of the world. "Guard the good treasure entrusted to you, with the help of the Holy Spirit living in us" (2 Timothy 1:14). Care for your soul. Life with God is a sacred trust. Your life of prayer is a mirror of God's likeness in you. When you guard the treasure that has been given into your trust, you are caring for your soul and the myriad of ways you make God's love tangible in your daily life. God's Holy Spirit, living in you, will help you every step along the way.

Resources

Books

Baldwin, Christina. *Life's Companion: Journal Writing as a Spiritual Quest.* New York: Bantam Books, 1990.
   This practical book will help readers discover the integral bond between spiritual experience and the everyday events that are the heart of a person's spiritual journey.

Bauman, Lynn C. *Ancient Songs Sung Anew: The Psalms as Poetry.* Telephone, Tx.: PRAXIS, 2008.
   This is an entirely new translation of the Psalms in the form of contemporary poetry that seeks the music as well as the meaning of the text. See www.praxisofprayer.com.

Bourgeault, Cynthia. *Chanting the Psalms: A Practical Guide with Instructional CD.* Boston: New Seeds Books, 2006.
   This book and CD provides a history of Christian psalmody and an appreciation of its place in contemplative prayer. The CD demonstrates basic techniques and easy melodies that any person can use.

Cotter, Jim. *Out of the Silence... Into the Silence: Prayer's Daily Round.* Harlech, UK: Cairns Publications, 2006.
   This is "an unfolding of prayers, psalms, and canticles for daily or occasional use" with a contemporary version of the psalms by Jim Cotter. See www.cottercairns.co.uk.

Easwaran, Eknath. *God Makes the Rivers to Flow: Passages for Meditation.* Petaluma: Nilgiri Press, 1982.

This book is an inspiring and useful collection of short passages from the sacred texts of the world's major religions, organized for meditation.

Hahn, Thich Nhat. *Present Moment Wonderful Moment: Mindfulness Verses for Daily Living.* Berkeley: Parallax Press, 1990.

This is an inspiring handbook of "mindfulness verses" that will help readers slow down and enjoy each moment of their lives.

Hahn, Thich Nhat. *The Long Road Turns to Joy: A Guide to Walking Meditation.* Berkeley: Parallax Press, 1996.

This little book offers instruction for walking just for the enjoyment of each step, each breath, and the sights and fragrances along the way, and tells how this simple practice can help us regain peace and serenity during difficult moments.

Hall, Thelma. *Too Deep for Words: Rediscovering Lectio Divina.* New York: Paulist Press, 1988.

This is a simple introduction to contemplative prayer as "consent to God's love." Sister Thelma provides an introduction to *lectio divina* (meditation on passages from the Bible) that is both inspiring and practical.

Hansen, Michael J., SJ, ed. *The Gospels for Prayer.* Notre Dame, Ind.: Ave Maria Press, 2003.

Hansen has divided each of the four gospels into short daily readings suitable for *lectio divina.* He begins the book with good advice about the practice of *lectio divina* and several suggestions for other ways to use the Bible in meditation. This book is both practical and wise.

Harris, Paul, ed. *Silence and Stillness in Every Season: Daily Readings with John Main.* Foreword by Lawrence Freeman, OSB. New York: Continuum, 1999.

This book provides a selection of daily readings and instruction from the writings of one of the most influential mentors of Christian meditation. John Main's

method of silent prayer draws on the ancient wisdom of
the Bible, the Hindu Upanishads, and the desert fathers.

Keating, Thomas, OCSO. *Open Mind, Open Heart.* New York:
Continuum, 1986.

Thomas Keating is a Cistercian monk who is very much
in touch with the heart of God and the needs of modern
society and who has inspired the renewal of the ancient
practice of Christian contemplative prayer. The form of
centering prayer he developed has given birth to a lay
movement teaching centering prayer through a network
called Contemplative Outreach. In this book Father
Keating describes the contemplative dimension of the
Christian gospel and responds to many questions
regarding the practice of contemplative prayer.

Kushner, Lawrence. *Honey from the Rock.* Woodstock, Vt.:
Jewish Lights Publications, 1990.

One of today's most articulate and contemplative rabbis
provides a poetic introduction to the Jewish mystical
path. Reflection on each passage in this book is an
experience of contemplative prayer.

Laird, Martin. *Into the Silent Land: The Practice of
Contemplation.* New York: Oxford University Press, 2006.

This is a simple, trustworthy guide into contemplative
prayer that emphasizes the role of the body, working
with a prayer word, and meeting distractions.

McDonnell, Patrick. *The Gift of Nothing.* New York: Little,
Brown and Company, 2005.

This book for children describes a cat's dilemma trying to
find a gift for a dog that does not need anything. It uses
very few words to articulate contemplative experience.

Merrill, Nan C. *Psalms for Praying: An Invitation to Wholeness.*
New York: Continuum, 2000.

A meditative version of all one hundred fifty psalms that
is true to the original vitality and honesty of the Psalter,
yet speaks to the hearts of modern women and men.

Muth. Jon J. *The Three Questions, Based on a Story by Leo Tolstoy.* New York: Scholastic Press, 2002.
A book for children demonstrating that without mindfulness and attention to the present moment we may never discover the things we desire most in life.

Norris, Gunilla. *Being Home: A Book of Meditations.* Photographs by Greta D. Sibley. New York: Bell Tower, 1991.
A beautiful collection of photographs of daily tasks in the home accompanied by a poetic meditation on each task.

Roth, Nancy. *The Breath of God.* New York: Seabury, 2006.
This delightful book brings together simple instructions in the basic prayer forms of the Christian tradition — contemplation, reflection, verbal prayer, and the prayer of action — with a theology that helps us embody our prayer in the daily round of family life, work, creativity, and community action.

Roth, Nancy. *Spiritual Exercises: Joining Body and Spirit in Prayer.* New York: Seabury, 2005.
This unique book reminds us that our bodies are sacred and can become an integral part of our daily praying. It offers a wealth of disciplines, from Pilates and Tai Chi to strength training and aerobics, all for the purpose of letting our bodies pray and become colleagues in our praying.

Schutz, Brother Roger. *Praying in Silence of Heart.* Chicago: GIA Publications, 2007.
This little book is a treasure of short prayers born in the silent prayer of Brother Roger of Taizé. Each prayer is suitable to begin or end a day or to include in a short morning or evening office.

The Spiritual Traveler series.
Paulist Press publishes a series of guides to sacred sites and peaceful places in urban and rural America. See especially *The Spiritual Traveler: New York City* by Edward F. Bergman, *The Spiritual Traveler: Boston and New England* by Jana Riess, and *The Spiritual Traveler: Chicago and Illinois* by Marilyn J. Chiat.

Vest, Norvene. *No Moment Too Small: Rhythms of Silence, Prayer, and Holy Reading.* Cambridge, Mass.: Cowley Publications, 1994.

This book by an Episcopal laywoman focuses on three of the foundations of the Benedictine way: silence, the exploration of scripture (*lectio divina*), and the daily hours of prayer. It makes these rich aspects of Benedictine monastic life accessible to all persons who seek God in the midst of busy and responsible lives. It also makes suggestions of passages for use in *lectio divina* and other forms of meditation.

CDs

Contemplative Prayer Forms. Shalem Institute for Spiritual Formation. www.shalem.org

This two-CD set offers a rich variety of opportunities to learn meditation and contemplative prayer. It is narrated by Tilden Edwards, with Marlene Maier, and includes an introduction to contemplative prayer by Gerald May.

In the Silence of the Word: A Carthusian Plainchant Meditation. Darton, Longman & Todd, 1998.

This is a collection of plainchant, readings from the Bible, and meditation from six monastic services by the Carthusian monks of Parkminster Abbey in England.

Let Go, Let Be: Chants for Meditation and Celebration. www.kelmusic.com

These chants by Kristopher E. Lindquist and sung by the choir of Grace St. Paul's Episcopal Church, Tuscon, are simple and easily learned by individuals or groups.

The Life of Jesus: A Meditation in Sound by Suzanne Toolan, RSM. OCP Publications.

Readings on the life of Jesus of Nazareth from the New Testament gospels, with piano improvisations by Suzanne Toolan, RSM, a gifted contemporary liturgical composer.

My Morning Prayer: Seven Daily Services for People on the Go.
Chicago: GIA Publications.

> This CD offers seven fifteen-minute services for morning
> prayer, combining a variety of hymns, chants, biblical
> reading, and prayers.

My Whole House. Johna Peterson. www.johnapeterson.com

> Voice and instrumental meditations from the Hebrew
> scriptures, the Christian gospels, medieval mystics, and
> Sufi poets.

*Sacred Improvisations: Piano Improvisations on Hymns, Spirituals,
and Chants.* Robert Koopman, OSB. Saint John's Abbey,
Collegeville, Minnesota.

> Father Koopman's solo improvisations provide a musical
> *lectio divina* on familiar hymns and chants. A great
> meditation.

Singing the Psalms by Cynthia Bourgeault. Available from
www.soundstrue.com.

> This four-CD set provides the history and significance of
> psalmody in the Christian contemplative tradition, and
> easy instructions for chanting the Psalms.

*Songs of Presence: Contemplative Chants for the New Millennium. A
Learning CD.* Chants composed by Lynn Bauman, David
Keller, Philip Roderick, and Suzanne Toolan, RSM.
www.praxisofprayer.com

> PRAXIS and the choir of All Saints' Episcopal Church
> in Corpus Christi, Texas, have created a learning CD of
> twenty-seven contemplative chants that are suitable for
> individual or group chanting. Presented first as a simple
> melody, voices and parts are then added to demonstrate
> how each chant can be expanded. The CD comes with a
> booklet insert with words and description of each chant.

DAILY MEDITATION WEBSITES

www.cottercairns.co.uk
> This website offers a variety of resources for daily prayer that use contemporary, inclusive language and are related to current issues and challenges of modern society.

www.explorefaith.org
> Spiritual guidance for anyone seeking a path to God, with helpful resources for various forms of prayer and meditation. It offers a fine weekly email newsletter (free) featuring prayers, reflections, and "tools for the journey."

www.gratefulness.org
> Provides a rich variety of resources that remind us of the fundamental importance of gratefulness in our lives. It is centered of the teaching of Brother David Steindl-Rast, OSB. It offers a free daily e-mail "Word for the Day."

www.HenriNouwen.org
> Daily meditations from the wisdom of Henri Nouwen, one of the most profound and influential Roman Catholic spiritual writers of the twentieth century.

www.prayasyougo.org
> Maintained by the Jesuits of Great Britain; provides daily podcasts. Prayerful meditations on scripture, complete with musical selections from different parts of the world, are provided in a well-structured ten-to-fifteen-minute program, Monday through Friday.

CHRISTIAN CONTEMPLATIVE PRAYER AND MEDITATION WEBSITES

The Center for Action and Contemplation
www.cacradicalgrace.org
> A Christian center forwarding the integration of social action and contemplation.

Contemplative Outreach
www.contemplativeoutreach.org
> Provides information about centering prayer groups
> within the Christian tradition, inspired by Thomas
> Keating, OCSO.

Questioning Minds
www.questioningminds.com
> A good website for seekers; designed to provide a
> community for people who are interested in deepening
> their spiritual lives but are uncomfortable with
> institutional religion. It is full of information about
> contemplative prayer practices, exploration of different
> faith traditions, and ways to stay grounded while
> pursuing spiritual growth, plus opportunities to discuss
> your beliefs, doubts, questions, and explorations.

World Community for Christian Meditation
www.wccm.org; www.johnmainprayer.com;
www.laycontemplative.org/world_community.html
> These websites provide information about Christian
> meditation groups inspired by John Main, OSB and
> Lawrence Freeman, OSB.

WEBSITES FOR MEDITATION
FROM OTHER RELIGIOUS TRADITIONS

The Blue Mountain Meditation Center
www.nilgiri.org
> Provides information about meditation from the Hindu
> tradition that includes wisdom from other traditions. The
> Center offers instruction and guidance in the Eight-Point
> Program of passage meditation and allied living skills
> developed by Eknath Easwaran.

Buddhist Network
www.buddhistnetwork.org
> Listings of opportunities for Buddhist meditation practice,
> dharma teaching, and local sangha groups near you.

The Chochmat Halev Center of Jewish Meditation
www.chochmat.org
 Provides information, courses, and training in Jewish
 meditation, a rich, varied, and little known tradition. This
 Center is helping to make meditation a part of
 mainstream Jewish spiritual practice.

The Sufi Conference
www.suficonference.org
 Provides information about Sufi meditation (a religious
 path within Islam). The Sufi Conference brings together
 different Sufi orders and lovers of God as an expression
 of oneness and love. The purpose of the Sufi Conference
 is to create a container for a spiritual energy, a frequency
 of divine love that is needed in the West for its spiritual
 evolution.

PRAYER SUPPLIES

Icons
www.skete.com
 The monks of St. Isaac of Syria Skete in Wisconsin
 provide an extensive selection of Orthodox Byzantine
 icons, as well as other devotional, gift, and media
 products, accessible to all and at very affordable prices.

Meditation Aids
www.praxisofprayer.com
 Praxis of Prayer offers a good selection of inexpensive
 meditation bells, rosaries (including the Anglican rosary),
 icons, and instructive chant CDs. The brass bowl
 meditation bells sit on cushions of silk and are struck by
 a mallet. Their tone is mellow and sustained. Depth of
 tone varies and is determined by size.

Meditation Cushions and Chairs
www.samadhicushions.com and zafu.com
 Pictures of meditation cushions and benches and two
 sources for purchasing them are found at these websites.

Endnotes

1. Unless otherwise noted, the sayings from the desert fathers quoted in this book are taken from Benedicta Ward's *The Desert Fathers: Sayings of the Early Christian Monks* (London: Penguin Books, 2003) and *The Sayings of the Desert Fathers* (Kalamazoo: Cistercian Publications, 1975).
2. Evelyn Underhill, "The Prayer of Silence," in *The Challenge*, vol. 3, no. 59 (1915).
3. John Main, *The Heart of Creation* (London: Darton, Longman & Todd, 1988), 29.
4. Pseudo-Macarius, Homily 1, in *The Fifty Spiritual Homilies and the Great Letter*, trans. and ed. George A. Maloney, SJ (New York: Paulist Press, 1992), 37–38.
5. Quoted in John Cassian, *The Conferences*, trans. Boniface Ramsey, OP (New York: Paulist Press, 1997), Conference 9, XII–XIV, 337–338.
6. Quoted by Thomas Merton in *Contemplative Prayer* (New York: Herder and Herder, 1969), 33.
7. Brother Roger, *Taizé: Trust, Forgiveness, Reconciliation* (London: Mowbray, 1986), 18.
8. See Vaclav Havel, "Democracy's Forgotten Dimension," *Journal of Democracy*, vol. 6, no. 2 (April 1995): 3–10, and "Politics, Morality, and Civility," in *Summer Meditations*, trans. Paul Wilson (New York: Vintage Books, 1992).
9. Christopher Alexander, *The Timeless Way of Building* (Oxford: Oxford University Press, 1979), 7, 19ff., 137ff.

10. This description is based on David K. Townsend, SJ, "Finding God in a Busy Day," in *Review for Religious*, vol. 50, no. 1 (January–February 1991): 43–63.

11. Henri Nouwen, *Bread for the World*, adapted for the Daily Meditation eLetter dated April 27, 2008.

12. Alexander Carmichael, *Carmina Gadelica: Hymns and Incantations* (Hudson, N.Y.: Lindisfarne Press, 1992), 93, 244.

13. Rumi, "The Shepherd's Care," in *In the Arms of the Beloved*, trans. Jonathan Starr (New York: Penguin Putnam, 1997), 59.

14. Raimon Panikkar, *The Experience of God: Icons of the Mystery* (Minneapolis: Fortress Press, 2006), 132–133.

15. This phrase is from Thomas Hand, SJ, *Meditation Matters*, a DVD produced by Mercy Center in Burlingame, California.

16. Sherry Ruth Anderson and Patricia Hopkins, *The Feminine Face of God* (New York: Bantam Books, 1992), 154.

17. Fiona Bowie and Oliver Davies, *Celtic Christian Spirituality: An Anthology of Medieval and Modern Sources* (New York: Continuum, 1995), 27.

18. Etty Hillesum, *An Interrupted Life: The Diaries and Letters of Etty Hillesum, 1941–1943*, intro. J. G. Gaarlandt, trans. Arnold J. Pomerans (New York: Pantheon Books, 1984).

19. I am indebted to W. Norman Pittenger, one of my most influential mentors in seminary, for this phrase taken from his book *Freed to Love: A Process Interpretation of Redemption* (Wilton, Conn.: Morehouse-Barlow, 1987).

CPSIA information can be obtained
at www.ICGtesting.com
Printed in the USA
FSOW01n0603211116
27537FS

9 780819 223197